Coyote Springs

Gail Odom West

Fulton Books
Meadville, PA

Published by Fulton Books 2024

ISBN 979-8-88982-911-9 (paperback)
ISBN 979-8-88982-912-6 (digital)

Printed in the United States of America

C HAPTER 1

Life had gotten back to normal for Della Butterfield. The past year had been such a nightmare for her. She never dreamed that when she had made the decision to start a new life, it would end up like it did. She had wanted a fresh start and made her choices. She drew a heavy sigh as she looked out her parlor window. She had been kidnapped by two men who were at war with each other. She shuddered.

Della's nightmares came nightly, waking her with fear and a heavy heart. She never told Sheriff Bronson the whole story. She knew that if she told of what Cal Potter had done to her, Travis would find out and would have killed Potter on the spot. She did not want that. Della loved Travis and knew that there was bad blood between both men. She kept silent and dealt with her own fears.

Nellie came into the room and brought Della out of her thoughts. Della turned and smiled. Nellie had been through as much herself. Cal Potter was an evil man. Nellie was asking Della if she wanted anything special for supper. Della stood up and told her that whatever she fixed would be fine. As Nellie was turning to leave, Della asked Nellie if she would help her do something. Nellie turned to look at Della and said she would. Della touched her on the shoulder and told her that she wanted to move into another room. Nellie understood and told her she would get Travis and some of the hands to get on it. Nellie headed back to the kitchen and started supper, then went to find Travis.

Come morning, the men were busy moving Della into another room. Travis made sure they had everything set up for Della. She wanted light and a new view. Travis made sure it was done the way Della wanted it.

Travis had been by Della's side every day since he had rescued her from Stewart Granger. Travis had found the secret of Coyote Springs, which was gold. This had given Della the leverage she needed to stand on her own. She was able to pay off her note at the bank and made improvements to Coyote Springs.

Travis completed moving Della and left to feed the livestock. He had a lot on his mind and blamed himself for what Della went through. He swore Potter was going to pay. The trial was coming up, and Travis felt confident that Potter would be found guilty. He could never get past the fact that Potter had killed his first true love. It had hardened his heart, yet here was Della who ripped it open again. He loved her, but he felt torn. To make a commitment to Della would be like forgetting the past. It made no sense, but that was how Travis felt. He had made a promise that Potter would pay, and he failed. Travis had failed Della because he was too afraid to come forward to tell Della how he felt.

Travis still had not made that step. Here he was with Della, and things were still the same. Travis was caught between revenge for the one he lost and commitment with the one he almost lost. The choice seems easy, but not for Travis. He knows that Della wants more, and he is afraid that he may lose her altogether. Travis had to search his heart for the right thing to do. He sighed and finished forking hay into the stalls.

Nellie and Sam had gotten married in the midst of all the chaos that Cal Potter and Stewart Granger had done. Della was so glad that Potter's plans of marrying her got foiled by Stewart Granger. Nellie and Sam were the perfect match. Della gave them a piece of property where they built a lovely home. They both are happy to be where they were and watch over Della.

Rosewood was also back to normal. Talk had died down, and everyone went about their business. Talk now was about Della and her newfound fortune. Rosewood was growing and wanted to leave the past behind. Rosewood wanted the trial to be over soon, and the town wanted a fresh start.

Sheriff Bronson had his hands full with Cal Potter in his jail. Deputy Eli Banks would spell the sheriff from time to time. Potter had a mouth on him, and it rubbed the sheriff wrong at times. Sheriff Bronson wandered over to see Doc from time to time to clear his head as he puts it. Doc would set up the checkerboard, and they would talk about different things.

Deputy Banks was a young man and green behind the years. Potter could work his way around the deputy when he needed something. There were times when the deputy would let a visitor in to see Potter when the sheriff was out of town. The deputy never told the sheriff about the visitor. He saw no harm in it.

The visitor was a woman and came every now and then. She made sure her face was hidden when she came to visit. She never stayed long, and their talk was muffled. The deputy should have been wary about these visits but never said a word.

Cal Potter was in the Rosewood jail for killing Gracie Muldoon. He claims he is innocent and had hired a lawyer, Joshua Wetherspoon, to prove it. Potter was mad at himself because he let his guard down. If Gracie had let him know what Granger was up to, he would have killed Granger, and after marrying Della, she would have an accident. He would then be able to take control of Coyote Springs and be a rich man. Potter hit the wall with his fist. The gold would have been his! Potter swore under his breath this time he would get it right.

Stewart Granger was also thinking. His life had changed in such a big way. He had become a madman and stooped so low as to kidnap Della. He had hired Cal Potter to help him get the land from Della. Granger shook his head. Della had looked so much like his wife, Julia, that he let his heart get in the way. Julia was a dark-headed beauty with hazel eyes and a sweet soul. He loved her very much, but he messed things up. He drank too much and was not there for her. She soon left him, and that was when he went mad.

Granger never would harm Della. He was confused. When he learned that Potter was going to marry Della, he flew into a rage. All he could see and think about was his Julia. In a way, he saved Della's life when he learned that Potter had killed his bride, thinking it was Della, but Gracie had changed places with Della. Granger knew that

Gracie was sweet on Potter if she only knew his evil side. Granger took a sip of his coffee and looked out his window. He knew he had to mend fences, and he was ready to get started.

The news of the upcoming trial traveled fast in saloons going from town to town. The newspapers were telling the story over and over for all who would listen. Rosewood would be overrun by reporters looking for a story. The papers had one reader who was very curious and had held the reader's interest. This was one trial that the reader wanted to see.

Doc was making sure that no one bothered Della, especially any reporters. He would not let Jim take them out to Coyote Springs. Most of the reporters would stay in town but soon left. They were waiting for the big day. Doc wanted to protect Della as much as possible. She needed her time before the trial started. He knew that it was going to be hard on her.

Jim Langford had ridden out to Coyote Springs to see Della. She had sent word to him. Della met him on the porch and invited him in. Jim followed Della into the house down the hall to the parlor. Once they were in the parlor and seated, Della told Jim that she had wanted to talk to him about the trial. Della went on to say that she wanted him to represent him. Jim Langford told her that he would be glad to. Jim told her that circumstances were in here favor and that trial would be over quickly.

Della asked him if she would have to testify. Jim looked at her and said that she may have to present what had happened to her. Della looked worried, and Jim quickly said that if she did have to testify, it would not be at the beginning. Della told him that she wanted Potter to pay. She did say that she did not want to press any charges against Stewart Granger or say anything about what happened. Jim took this in stride and told her that Potter was on trial, and he was the only one they would deal with. Jim asked Della other questions, which she answered the best she could. Jim was taking notes and letting Della know that she could take her time. After a long while, he had plenty of information to work with.

Della soon showed him out. He told her that he got word that the trial was going to be the first of the coming month. Della stopped in her tracks. Jim asked her if she was all right. She said that she was and that she was glad that the trial was soon. Jim said the sooner they got over this, the better she would be able to rest. Jim shook her hand and told her not to worry and that if she needed anything, he would ride out again. Soon, Della was watching Jim Langford head out the gate.

Travis had seen Jim Langford leaving and came up to the house to see what was going on. Della told him that she had hired him as her lawyer, in which Travis said that he was a good one. Della turned to sit in a rocking chair with Travis taking a chair next to her. She told him that the trial would start at the beginning of the next month. Travis was quiet for a moment, then said, "The sooner, the better." Della turned and was about to say something to Travis when Nellie came out. Della told her the news, and she took her apron and wiped her brow. She also was glad that it would be over soon.

Della never got the chance to talk with Travis because Sam had come up, and the four were soon talking about other things. Conversation was light with a hint of wanting to say more but held off. Della became quiet as she stole glances at Travis. Her heart was aching to be in his arms and for him to tell her again how much he loved her. Yet he had not. Was it something that she did? Was it what had happened that had changed him? Will she ever have the strength to tell him the truth?

Della came out of her thoughts in time to hear Travis saying that he was going to check the mine. The gold mine was a work in progress. Silas Reed Travis's pa was the overseer of the mine. There was still much to do. Travis and Sam had been helping with the building of a house for Silas and Autumn and other outbuildings. Della knew that the mine was an escape for Travis. She sighed.

Autumn saw her son riding up. She could tell he was troubled. She did not say anything but had an idea of what was going on. Silas hollered at Travis and told him he was just in time. She waved him on and went back to her work. Silas had the last beam to put in place and needed Travis to help. Both men stood back and admired their work. Autumn walked up and put her arms around her husband and turned to her son. She told him she was worried about him. Travis just shrugged it off and went back to work helping his pa.

She was a wise woman who listened and watched those around her. The first time that Autumn met Della, she knew that she was the right one for her son. Della had a spirit that connected with her son. Travis is blinded by revenge and cannot see how much love Della has for him. She knows that her son says he loves Della, but at what depth? Love runs deep, and sometimes, it is tested in ways that are beyond anyone's control. Autumn knows that Travis will be tested and will have to make his decision and live with it before it is too late. Travis stayed until the sun was setting before he headed back to Coyote Springs. Nellie was setting the table when he came in. Della came in behind her with a tray. It was not long before Sam joined them and sat down to enjoy Nellie's cooking. Supper was noticeably quiet to the point where Nellie had an idea that something was wrong. She groaned inside and thought, *Here we go again.*

After supper, Travis asked Della if she would like to go for a walk, to which she said yes. They excused themselves and left the room. Travis took Della's hand as they walked along the rim of the creek. The air smelled of wild roses, and the moon was full. They seemed to walk for hours before Travis said anything. He stopped and turned her toward him and held her close. Travis whispered in her ear that he had something to say to her. Della stood back and held her breath waiting.

Travis looked at Della and was acting like what he had to say was difficult. Della stepped back and gave him room. He told her that he loved her and wanted to protect her. She said I love you too. She went toward him, but Travis took her by the arms. He told her that it would be best if he kept his distance until after the trial was over. He went on to say that he must deal with Cal Potter in his own way. Travis was saying that he had things from his past that he needed to take care of before he could start over. Della stepped back, not believing what she was hearing.

Della looked at Travis and saw from the look in his eyes that he was still holding on to the past and blinded by the revenge that was taking hold of him. She wondered if he ever really loved her. He said he did, but he even sounded unsure of himself. She spoke softly to Travis when she told him she understood and was sorry that she was making his life difficult. Della went on telling Travis that she would go on with her life and leave him to deal with his past and that one day she hoped that he would be at peace. When she finished, Della turned and left Travis standing with an agonizing look on his face. Della walked away with tears streaming down her face.

Della made it back to the house and went straight to her room, where she flung herself on the bed and cried her eyes out. Travis had stayed longer before he came to the house. He went into his room a very somber man wondering if he had done the right thing.

In the weeks ahead, Della and Travis spoke to each other but nothing more. Travis continued his work and looked after Della from a distance. Nellie and Sam knew that things had changed. They were hoping that the coming trial would come and go quickly. Della ached for Travis daily but knew that her love for him would not die. She prayed that one day Travis would come back to her, but for now, he had to deal with his own demons. When would that day come?

Potter was lying on his bunk in his cell looking out the small window at a portion of the sky. He snickered and turned in his bunk. He was feeling low that his plan had not worked. He almost got away with it. Della was a nice-looking gal and had spunk. Then there was Travis. He never knew that he would ever run into him again. How long it had been.

He had received a telegram in New Orleans that a rancher in Texas wanted to hire him to do a little job. Potter was for hire, and if the price were right, he would get the job done. He remembered one of his first jobs, he stepped out of the stagecoach in a dusty small town. He had met the rancher who laid out his plan of attack. Now Potter loved women, and this job he came to enjoy. The victim was Beth. She was the daughter of Slim and Peg, squatters on land that the rancher wanted.

Seemed like yesterday when he met the young Beth, never knowing that she had a young buck hot on her heels. Potter remembered how easy it was to woo Beth and her parents. They did not know what hit them until Travis started nosing around. The rancher paid handsomely for Potter to get the land for him. Beth was just the icing on the cake. Travis fought hard, but Potter was one step ahead of him. Potter remembers when a showdown between them went bad. Beth had run out into the street just as he had fired at Travis.

Beth fell to the ground. Travis was like a raging bull. Travis lunged at Potter and cut him with a knife. Potter hit Travis hard, knocking him to the ground. Potter remembers seeing Travis crawling to Beth and holding her as she died. Potter sighed. He rubbed the old scar and swore he would get back at Travis. Now he was in jail because of Travis Reed. He had it all until Stewart Granger went crazy on him. Potter had a feeling all along that there was more to Coyote Springs, and finding the gold was it. He was not finished yet. He had planned well, and things were about to get interesting. He was going to sit back and enjoy the ride. Potter turned over and finally went to sleep.

CHAPTER 2

The air was thick with cigarette smoke. Voices were getting louder, trying to be heard over the din. Judge William Cartwright slammed his gavel onto the table before him. He looked over to Sheriff Tom Bronson and told him to close the bar. The judge addressed the crowd and told them to settle down, or he would have them thrown out. He cleared his throat and asked that the prisoner be brought in.

Sheriff Bronson stepped into the adjourning room and came out with Cal Potter and Deputy Banks in tow. The trial of Cal Potter was about to begin.

The whole town of Rosewood had been dreading this day. It had taken some time for the town to start over. The whole Cal Potter and Stewart Granger deal had been a great blow to this small town. Yet justice had to be served for all concerned. Rosewood had changed into a better town and was ready for the change.

Della Butterfield had awoken that morning. She got dressed and went down to see Nellie. Travis was coming into the house to see if Della was ready to go. The house was quiet. Old wounds were going to be opened, and Della felt a sense of dread. She turned to Travis and said she was ready with Nellie close behind.

The ride into town was a quiet one. Both women were looking off into the distance, each thinking about that awful day, the day Gracie died.

Della remembered that day in like a trance. She had been so heartsick and ashamed of herself that she had opened herself up to Cal Potter. She was easy prey. She had been a saloon girl and had worked for Ms. Nancy at the Desert Rose. Della had only been ten when her parents brought her to Texas. They ended up in Rosewood when her mother had gotten sick then died. Ms. Nancy had taken her in. Soon after, her daddy had drunk himself to death. Della wanted a fresh start and had bought the property from the Bagwells.

Nellie Montgomery, Ms. Nancy's cook, had decided to come along with Della. The two women had gotten Coyote Springs off the ground and were doing very well until Cal Potter had come to town, then all hell broke loose! Della heaved a sigh as she came back to the present. Travis was turning the rig toward Doc's. Doc came out to greet them. Jim West, Doc's driver, took the reins from Travis and told him he would see to the horses. Travis thanked him and helped the ladies down. Della dusted off her dress and turned to give Doc a big hug. He had been like a father to her. Doc patted her on the back and asked if she was ready. Della nodded and turned to walk toward the Desert Rose with Nellie close behind.

Rosewood did not have a courthouse as such, so the sheriff would use the Desert Rose from time to time to hold a trial. This was a big one. People from all around had come into Rosewood. Everyone had their own opinions and was not scared to voice them. The saloon was so packed that it was getting hard to breathe. Ms. Nancy asked Jed, the bartender, to open the back door to let a breeze come through. About that time, Della walked in, and the room got even quieter.

Her eyes looked around the room until she saw Ms. Nancy and then walked in her direction. Her back was straight, head held high as she came to sit by Ms. Nancy. Nellie was close behind and sat behind both women. Travis decided to stand near Jed behind the bar. He did not want to get too close to Cal Potter. Cal Potter was taking everything in. His eyes followed Della like a cat ready to strike. He was reeling in rage when Della and Travis walked into the room. He darted his eyes away when he saw Travis go behind the bar. Potter looked around the room until he found what he was looking for. His face formed a thin smile. He was not worried at all.

Judge Cartwright again slammed his gavel on the table. Sheriff Bronson stood beside the bench and told all in the room to remain quiet. The judge looked at the accused and his lawyer, Joshua

Wetherspoon, and asked if he was ready to start. Wetherspoon nodded and stood up; he pushed his horn-rimmed glasses back on his nose. He addressed the judge that he was and that he was going to prove that Cal Potter was not responsible for the murder of Gracie Muldoon or the kidnapping of Della Butterfield!

The room erupted in a loud uproar. Judge Cartwright banged his gavel on the table, shouting for order, or he was going to have the room cleared. Everyone sat back down and whispered. Della looked across at Travis who had a look of hate in his eyes, for he had not taken his eyes off Potter. Wetherspoon continued; he stated that Mr. Potter was pushed to draw his gun when Travis had entered the room. Mr. Potter felt threatened, and his gun misfired. Wetherspoon went on to say that Della Butterfield was engaged to Mr. Potter and that she was a willing participant.

A murmur went through the room. Wetherspoon continued and said that it was Gracie Muldoon who fooled Cal Potter by believing she was Della. It was a tragic mistake. Cal Potter was innocent. Again, the room was buzzing. The judge looked across the room, and it became quiet. He told the court that he had heard the defendant's side; now he would hear the prosecution's side.

Jim Langford stood up and looked around the room. He turned to look at Potter and said that he would prove that Cal Potter was guilty of the murder of Gracie Muldoon and the pain and suffering that Della Butterfield and Nellie Montgomery went through by the hands of Cal Potter. A cheer went through the room but soon was quiet. Langford also said that not only Cal Potter was to blame, but also Stewart Granger was the one who paid him to approach Della for his own selfish benefit.

Jim Langford went on to say that Cal Potter turned the tables on Stewart Granger and wanted everything for himself. Potter knew Granger was a sick man and took advantage of him. Jim Langford walked over to the table where Potter had a blank look. Potter jumped when Langford hit the table with his fist and said that he was guilty and would rot in prison! Potter was about to come up out of his chair but was stopped by his lawyer, Wetherspoon.

Judge Cartwright hit his gavel to the table again to regain order. The air was thick with anticipation. This was going to be a long trial. The judge said now that the prosecution had concluded his statement that the lawyer for the defendant would call his first witness. Wetherspoon stood up and called Stewart Granger to the stand. The room was holding its breath as Granger walked through the front door of the saloon. He walked straight up to the witness stand. Sheriff Bronson asked him to raise his right hand up and swear on the Bible that he would tell the whole truth and nothing but the truth. Stewart Granger said that he would set the record straight, and then he sat down. Della had been holding her breath for what seemed eternal. She looked at Granger and was surprised that he was looking back at her. In the brief glance, she saw that she had nothing to fear from him anymore. He seemed changed. He turned his gaze to Wetherspoon who was asking him what his name was. Granger replied that he was Stewart Granger and was owner of the Triple S. Wetherspoon asked him if he had hired Cal Potter. Granger said that he did, but if he knew that Potter was going to double-cross him, he would have shot him dead! The judge told the witness to answer the questions that were asked and no more. Granger told the judge he would.

The room settled down again, and Wetherspoon asked the question again. This time, Granger said he did. Wetherspoon turned to investigate the courtroom and asked what his reason was for hiring Potter. Granger took a moment and cleared his throat. He said that he wanted Coyote Springs. Wetherspoon turned and said, "Was that all?" Granger stared into the lawyer's eyes and said no. Wetherspoon walked up to Granger and said, No? Then what, pray tell, did he want?" Granger said, "Della Butterfield." The courtroom erupted again.

Judge Cartwright slammed his gavel, demanding order in the room. Della had shrunk in her chair. She was remembering what Granger had put her through. She stood up and was making her way to the door for fresh air. Travis was coming around the bar to follow her. She was at the door when she caught sight of someone familiar, but kept walking.

Travis asked if she was okay. Della said, "I just needed some air." Soon she turned to go back into the room. Della sat beside Ms. Nancy again and patted her knee and told her she was okay. Della looked toward Granger as he was being questioned. He admitted he had hired Potter and that he was hell-bent in having Della. He said that he had been so overwrought on losing his wife, Julia, that he did not know what he was doing. Della was so much like Julia that he just lost reason. Wetherspoon was shaking his head. He looked at Granger and said, "Is it not true that Potter double-crossed you because he had fallen in love with Della Butterfield, and you were so furious with revenge that you kidnapped Della on their wedding day?" Granger just looked at Wetherspoon and said yes.

Wetherspoon said, "I have no more questions for this witness." The judge asked Jim Langford if he had any questions. Langford stood up and said yes. He then walked around from behind his table and stood in front of Granger. He looked at Granger and asked him how he was feeling. Granger shifted in his chair and said that he felt fine. Langford went on to say that he knew that Stewart Granger had been a tormented man. He asked Granger what made him come back to his senses.

Granger held his head up and said, "The day Gracie was buried." Langford asked him why that had changed him. He said that after he had spent time in jail for what he had done to Della, he had time to think. He had been holding hatred in his heart for quite some time. He said he finally came to terms with the reason his Julia left him. He stopped for a moment; Langford told him to go on. Granger said that he stood by Gracie's grave knowing that he was just as guilty for her death. He never wanted anyone to get hurt. He said that in his madness, he had thought Della was his Julia. He looked at Della and said that it came to him that if Gracie had not changed places with Della, then it would have been his Julia lying there. Granger said that he vowed on Gracie's grave that Potter would pay.

The courtroom erupted again; the judge told the witness to hold his tongue. The room was trying to quiet down. Potter was glaring at Granger. Langford said he had no more questions; the judge asked the witness to step down. Granger stood up and walked out of the courtroom.

Judge Cartwright slammed his gavel on the table and said it was getting close to lunch; court was adjourned until two o'clock. Sheriff Bronson told Deputy Banks to take the prisoner back to the jail. Potter stood up and just smirked as the deputy led him out of the room. The judge asked the sheriff about the statement that Granger had made. The sheriff said that there was bad blood between the two, but that Granger had come to terms with his wrongdoing.

CHAPTER 3

Ms. Nancy had invited Della and Travis to lunch with her. Nellie and Sam were already helping to get the table set. Doc had stopped for a moment before going with Ms. Nancy. He thought he heard something outside; he was not too wrong.

Deputy Banks was coming back into the saloon from the side door and slumped to the floor. He had blood gushing from the back of his head. Doc rushed to him and caught the deputy. Banks was saying that Potter escaped. Someone had come up behind him, and then he was out. Sheriff Bronson had seen his deputy come through the door; he went out in a flash. There was no sign of Potter. The judge told the sheriff to get a posse and go after him. Travis inwardly groaned. Della said that she may have seen someone who would have helped Potter. The sheriff asked her who did she thought it was. She said, "The Smiths, Bob and Polly."

The deputy was being bandaged by Doc. He said he thought he had heard a woman's voice and that they had headed east out of town. Travis told the sheriff he was going to Coyote Springs and warn Silas, and then he would catch up with them. The sheriff told him to make it quick; both men were soon out the door.

Judge Cartwright told Doc that he hoped that Potter would be caught before sundown. Doc looked up and told him that no one would be safe until Potter was caught. He turned and looked at Della and met her eyes. He knew she was scared and had every right to be.

Jim Langford came into the Desert Rose when he heard about Potter escaping. The judge was walking into the room as Jim entered the saloon. The judge told him what happened. He also wanted to know where Wetherspoon was, then he walked in. Joshua Wetherspoon was wet behind the ears, and Potter was his first client. Wetherspoon swore that he knew nothing of Potter's escape or even helping him. The judge gave him a stern warning and told him that he better be telling the truth, or he would be spending a long time in prison.

Cal Potter was hiding under some blankets in the back of a wagon. Bob and Polly Smith had succeeded in getting Potter out. Bob turned the wagon on to a small trail and pulled up the team. He quickly ran back and put brush in the path's way. They had picked a nice wooded area. Bob told Potter that all was clear. Cal Potter made his way out of the wagon. Polly had the key to unlock the handcuffs. Potter was soon free. Bob climbed up into the wagon to retrieve a gun and a bottle of whiskey and handed them to Potter who was more than grateful.

Potter asked if they had been followed. Bob laughed and said they had slipped out quietly since everyone was still at the trial. Potter asked if everything was ready, which Polly spoke up and said that she had gotten what he needed and would be able to hold up for a while. Potter just shook his head in agreement. On his face, he had a far-away look. Soon they loaded back up on the wagon and headed off.

Travis had lit out as fast as he could to head off to his pa, Silas Reed. Travis was worried and had to get to Coyote Springs. Silas and Autumn, Travis's parents, were the overseers of the gold mine. Silas had a good team of men that he trusted working for him. They were getting ready to go back to work when Travis came riding in hard.

Silas could tell by the look on Travis's face that something was wrong, terribly wrong, and he soon found out. Travis told his pa to tell the men to be on the lookout that there was no telling what Potter was up to. Travis went on to say that he would be after him and Della. Silas told him to be careful and to watch his back. Travis nodded and rode off. Autumn had come out of the house and saw Travis. She knew that there was trouble. She turned and went back into the house. Silas turned and went to the house to let Autumn know what had happened. He shook his head as he walked.

Now back at Rosewood, the posse had left out in the direction of Cal Potter, hoping to catch up with him. The Smiths had a good head start. The posse caught up with Travis at Coyote Springs, but no one had seen any sign of the Smiths or Potter. Sheriff Bronson said that they must have held up somewhere. Travis was just as puzzled.

Della and Nellie were still with Ms. Nancy back at the Desert Rose. She was worried and knew that he was an evil man. She never told the whole story about her ordeal with the man. She was afraid, very afraid. She thought of Travis. He had been by her side ever since he rescued her from Stewart Granger. Yet ever since the night of their last walk, things had changed. Della was lost in thought, telling herself that one day, Travis would come back to her.

Ms. Nancy brought Della out of her thoughts, saying that with Potter on the lam, she needed to stay in town. Della told her no. She was going home; she went on to say that no matter where she was, Potter would find her and Travis. Ms. Nancy patted her knee and did not say another word; she knew Della was right. Nellie excused herself to find Sam to bring their buggy. Soon, Sam and the women were on their way to Coyote Springs.

Sheriff Bronson and the posse had gone as far as they could but with no lead on where Potter went. They came upon Stewart Granger and filled him in on what had happened. He was not surprised. He looked at Travis and told him to be careful. Potter had a score to settle. Travis said that he was ready. Granger shifted in his saddle and told him, "You may be ready, but with Della in the middle, it would be messy." Travis just sat back and cringed inside. Granger said he would keep the sheriff posted and have his hands on guard. Besides, he had a score to settle, too, and he turned to ride off. The sheriff and the posse turned to head toward town.

The Smiths pulled up the wagon. They had arrived at the place where Potter would hold up for a while. Potter looked around and grinned as he helped them unload the wagon. Soon Potter was thinking he was going to strike, and this time, he was going to win. He told the Smiths to clear out and cover their tracks, to also get out of Texas as soon as possible. Bob said that they had done what he asked, and now he wanted to know where the rest of the money was. Potter told them where they would be able to get the rest of the money owed to them. He also told them that he would hunt them down and kill them both if they double-crossed him. They assured him that he could count on them, and they were soon gone.

Potter watched them leave. He was a man that always tied up loose ends. He knew that the Smiths would never tell where he was. In fact, they would not be able to talk at all. He grinned despite himself and got busy securing his hideout. He had enough food and ammo to last a while. He had all the time in the world.

The sheriff made it back to town with the posse and Travis in tow. He headed over to the Desert Rose to see Della but learned they had already left for home. Travis got a fresh horse from the livery and headed back to Coyote Springs. He had so much on his mind, and the old wounds had opened again. He loved Della and wanted to make her his wife, hoping to make this possible after the trial. Now Travis was very uncertain of their future. If Travis only knew of what lay ahead.

Sam had made good time getting the women back to Coyote Springs. He had been thinking all the way home. Sam and Nellie had their own home next to the boardinghouse because Nellie wanted to be close to Della. Sam wanted to keep Nellie safe, so he knew he always had to be on extra guard. He pulled up to the porch and helped the women to step down He soon turned the buggy around and headed to the barn. He saw Travis riding through the gate, heading to the barn, so he quickened his pace.

Travis pulled up outside the barn as Sam came around with the buggy. He asked if they had found Potter. Travis said there was no sign of him or the Smiths. Sam shook his head and said, "We will always have to be on guard." Travis agreed. Travis told Sam, "We have to tell the women to be prepared." Sam thought for a moment and laughed. He told Travis about one of his many visits to Coyote Springs when he saw Della and Nellie with pistols strapped to their waists. Travis had to laugh, too; he was remembering the look in Della's eyes that day that made him love her more.

Nellie had gone into the kitchen to prepare a light supper, and they would have it on the porch. It was a nice evening, and the coyotes were playing along the ridge. Soon the two couples were enjoying their meal and one another's company. Silas and Autumn had ridden out for a visit. Conversation led to what they were all going to do with Potter on the loose. Travis told the women that they would have to arm themselves again. Nellie laughed. She said that she already was and held up her apron. Everyone laughed. Della said that she would be ready also. Autumn noticed that Della had more on her mind. It showed on her face, and it was eating her up inside. Autumn could tell that her son could not see the pain in her eyes. He was only concerned about Potter and getting his revenge on him. She sighed.

Stewart Granger had gone back to his ranch after his conversation with the sheriff and Travis. He paced in his living room for several hours before he would drink himself into oblivion, but now, he was different. He had to work hard to make things right. The Triple S was severely damaged from all his terrible doings. He lost several good hands. He was slowly gaining the trust of the ones that were left. Cal Potter was his problem. He had hired him because of his fixation with Della, so it was his responsibility to put an end to it for good.

Granger wanted to make everything right again with Della and explain to her how sorry he was for causing her so much pain. Would Della allow this? He would try, and hopefully, she would listen. He came out of his thoughts when Ray Cheekman stepped into the room. Granger turned. Granger told him that Potter had escaped and that the Triple S needed to be on guard. Cheekman said that he had heard the news and had already passed along the info to the other hands. Granger made it clear to Cheekman that he was to be the only one to find Potter. "Potter is my problem, and I will deal with it." Cheekman nodded his head and left.

Now Potter was settling down in his hideout. He was pleased despite himself. As he looked up into the clear night sky and drifted off to sleep, he would go exploring and set his revenge into play. He sighed as he closed his eyes and was snoring peacefully.

Sheriff Tom had gone home and was trying not to let Potter's escape get to him. Deputy Banks was doing better even though he got knocked on the head badly. He was in deep thought when his wife, Sue, touched his arm. He was startled but looked into his wife's eyes and saw that she was worried. He took her by the hand and told her not to worry. She gave him a halfway smile. She knew her husband well and knew he would not rest until Cal Potter was caught! She sighed, for soon he was lost in thought again. He knew that the days ahead would be tough. Where was Potter? Sheriff Tom stared out the window into the night. He had to be found soon. He had to get the "wanted" posters out and hope some bounty hunter would haul him in. Potter could be anywhere.

The town had settled down for the night. The trial had started out with a bang. Now Cal Potter had escaped and almost killed Deputy Banks. Everyone was on edge and would have many sleepless nights. Rosewood thought it was going to get back to normal, but it was not meant to be.

Doc was standing outside, finishing his evening pipe, and turned to tell Jim, his driver, that he would have to be more careful when he drives any new lodgers out to Coyote Springs. Jim said that he would be and would keep his eyes out for sure. Doc tapped his pipe against his hand, and soon both men turned in to call it a night.

The coyotes continued their play up on the ridge of Coyote Springs. They had no care in the world. Silas and Autumn had ridden back to the mine. He wanted to make sure there was a guard posted every night until Potter was caught. Autumn listened to the coyotes and smiled despite herself; she knew that the call of the coyotes had brought Travis to Della. Time will tell when all is set right. She knew her son was strong, like his father, stubborn like a mule at times. She knew she would have to give her son a push, whether he liked it or not.

Silas felt restless despite himself. They had always traveled from place to place. It was Autumn who wanted to stay put awhile. He had learned a long time ago to do what she wanted because she was always right. Silas sighed and turned toward their home. Soon they were drifting off to sleep with the sound of the coyotes.

Bob and Polly Smith had made good time in leaving Texas. They headed straight to Louisiana to meet up with the rest of their money. The Smiths have always been enterprising. That was why Potter had hired them. They had gotten rid of the wagon and changed their route several times. They had sworn to Potter that no one would find him.

It was in the days to come that the Smiths had checked into a hotel in New Orleans but was never seen again. The desk clerk had gone up to their room the next morning to check on the couple. There had been complaints from another guest. The clerk knocked but no answer. He took his key and opened the door. The room had been turned upside down. He stepped in to take a closer look at the damage. When he walked across the room, he caught a glimpse of something from the corner of his left eye, he turned and saw a foot. When he stepped closer, he saw the still body of Bob Smith, and lying next to him was his wife, Polly, both dead. The desk clerk made a mad dash out the door straight to the local sheriff's office. Cal Potter's fate was sealed. No one would know where he was, and he liked it that way.

The sheriff walked over to the Rosewood Inn to see Judge Cartwright. The sheriff saw the judge having coffee, so he walked over to join him. The judge set his cup down when Sheriff Tom approached him. He told the judge that they still have not found Potter; the judge just sat back and shook his head. He told the sheriff that he hoped he would catch him soon. Sheriff Tom told him he would do all he could.

Judge Cartwright said he was leaving town and would be back when Potter was in custody. He was waiting for both the lawyers to tell them also. Sheriff Tom excused himself as Jim Langford and Joshua Wetherspoon walked in. The judge went and met them in the foyer and told them the news that the sheriff had told him. He also said that he was leaving town. He looked at Wetherspoon and told him that if he had any knowledge of where Potter was, it would be in his best interest if he turned him in. Wetherspoon again said that he had nothing to do with his escape but would do all he could to help find Potter. The judge looked at both men and turned to leave.

C H A P T E R 4

It was business as usual for Coyote Springs. Jim West was steadily bringing new boarders out. He enjoyed his daily rides out to Coyote Springs, which gave him a chance to keep his eyes and ears open.

Della was keeping herself busy. She had to keep her mind off things. She was fighting within herself over the secret that she kept from Travis. Her love for him was strong, and when she was near him, she could feel his heartbeat and knew the very smell of him. Her heart longed for the day that they would marry. She lost herself in thought with his arms around her. She sighed. Would that be enough?

Travis, on the other hand, was feeling his own torture. His love for Della was so strong, he felt like he was going to explode. She was his life and his soul. After he had rescued her from the hands of Granger, he saw a change in her. He felt that something was going on inside her that she was dealing with. He never asked her about what really happened. He respected her too much. He knew in time she would tell him. His love for her had grown, but he still could not make a commitment to her. Now with Potter on the run, he was not going to even try.

Silas had his hands full at the mine. Everyone was busy trying to do their work and watch out for Potter. Travis pitched in to stand guard as much as possible. The mine had a nice vein of gold. Silas had hired men that he knew and trusted. The driver was known as Jay Blackfoot. He was a big man and talked little, not a man you would want to go against. Silas also hired a Cherokee, Sparrow, who was Autumn's brother. He had a keen eye and hit his target head-on.

The miners were Bo Jackson, Dan Fields, Ty Nettles, and Jeremy Stone. All good and trusted men. Silas had chosen well.

Cal Potter awoke with a purpose; he was well hid and could easily have a small campfire without being noticed. He sat back and sipped his coffee, planning his next move, and knew he had to be careful. He thought of Coyote Springs and gritted his teeth. He could have kicked himself for not being the one to find the secret of Coyote Springs. Gold, Della Butterfield a rich woman, quite different from being a saloon girl. He took another sip of coffee and lit a cigarette, took a deep drag, and slowly let it out. He was thinking hard. He had jumped too quickly this time. He was going to take his time.

Sheriff Tom had made "wanted" posters for the capture of Cal Potter. The sheriff walked to his window in deep thought. He finally concluded that Cal Potter had not left Texas and was close by. He knew in a matter of time that Potter would make his move. Sheriff Tom would be waiting for that move.

Nellie had been watching Della, seeing her friend retreat into herself. Nellie knew that Della had been through a lot with Granger and Potter. Nellie herself had been locked up nightly by Potter. Lord only knows what Della went through. She did know that it was destroying her friend. Nellie decided she would talk to Della and get to the bottom of things, and it would be soon.

Della, on the other hand, was considering talking to Nellie also. She knew Nellie would not betray her secret, yet she shook despite herself. Cal Potter was out there somewhere, and she was not safe nor Travis. She hung her head in her hands and sobbed.

Nellie thought she heard something and was coming out of the kitchen when she heard a knock at the door. Nellie thought that strange since everyone usually walks in. She went to the door, drying her hands on her apron, and was surprised to see Stewart Granger standing in the doorway with his hat in hand. Nellie composed herself and asked him what he wanted. He cleared his throat and asked to speak with Della. Della, by this time, had stepped out of her office and told Granger to please come in and that she would talk with him.

Stewart Granger followed Della into the parlor with Nellie close behind. Della asked him if he would like some refreshment, and he said, "Coffee would be nice." Nellie went to prepare the coffee as Della asked Granger to have a seat. He was uncomfortable, but he was determined to have a few words with Della.

Della asked him about the reason for his visit. He said that for quite some time, he had wanted to speak to her to apologize for all the wrongdoing that he had put her through. Nellie walked in with a tray of coffee and cookies. Della told her she was fine, that Mr. Granger wanted a private conversation. Nellie understood and left quietly.

Della poured their coffee and told him to go on. Granger took a sip of his coffee and was more relaxed by her manner. He told her that it was his fault that he hired Cal Potter to scare her into selling Coyote Springs to him. Granger went on to say that he had a feeling that there was gold on the land. He admitted that he had been searching for years but could never find it. Granger told Della that he felt obligated to her because of all the pain he caused. He cleared his throat and went on to say that he overstepped his bounds because of his fixation on her that she was so much like his beloved Julia. Della listened and watched Granger's face. She knew this was hard for him, and he was telling the truth. She knew he was still grieving for his wife and that he was in turmoil.

Granger told Della that there was no excuse in the way he treated her and what she went through with Cal Potter. Della put her cup down and told Granger what he did to her was the love he had for Julia. Della told him that she saw how much he loved Julia and that she reminded him of her. She went on to say that she knew he would not have hurt her because of that love. She went on to say, "In a way, when Potter had double-crossed you to marry me, you were thinking that he was taking your Julia away, and you came to rescue me." She went on to say, "In your mind, you had our Julia back and never wanted her to leave again."

Stewart Granger had gotten quiet. He knew she understood. Granger went on to say that when Gracie approached him about switching places before the wedding, he thought it was a great pay-back to Potter. Granger said that Gracie always listened to him every night talking about his Julia. He said she never complained and that he liked her. He said that he did not have any clue that Potter was going to kill her. Della told him that she knew he was going to kill her. Granger had a look of surprise. Della stood and refilled their cups. She sat back in her seat. Granger asked Della why she thought that. Della said, "Potter knew that you wanted Coyote Springs. That was why you had hired him, so the only way he would take it from you was to marry me." Della looked at Granger and said, "Gracie saved my life that day. I would have been the one killed that day. Cal Potter would have it all."

Della took a sip of coffee as Granger was letting this sink in. Della's hands were shaking slightly, so she set her cup down. She gathered her composure and said, "I have not told this to Nellie or Travis." She looked at Granger and said that Cal Potter was a very cruel man. She had tears in her eyes as she told Granger how Potter would leave the women alone in the house and take their horses so they could not leave. Della told Granger that Potter would lock Nellie in her room nightly, so she would not hear her cry out.

Della said she had gotten sick and was out of her mind at times. Potter would come into her room at night and tie her hands and feet to the bed frame. She said he would sit there for hours, his hands all over, sometimes beating her, telling her that when he was finished with her that no one would want her. Della said she tried talking to him, but he was like a madman at times. She learned to lie still and take whatever he did to her. Della said that by the next morning when he untied her, she was so weak and had to hide all the bruises on her body. Stewart Granger was clinching the cup he was holding with a sense of sickness in his stomach.

Della told Granger that Potter was going to kill her on their wedding night after he had his fun with her and send her dead body to Travis. He wanted to see Travis go mad and that Potter was going to make sure Granger was taken care of for good. Della said that she could not tell Travis any of this, for she was afraid of what he might do. Granger asked Della why she told him. Della said because of all the people she knew that he would understand how his love for Julia is as deep as her love for Travis. She went on to say Cal Potter has no ounce of love or compassion in him. No matter how much pain he inflicts, it is no match for the love two people have for each other.

Della told Granger that she had forgiven him long ago. She told him that she was glad that he came to see her and that she considered him her friend. Granger's eyes misted for a moment, and he said that he was her friend and that her secret was safe with him. Della told Granger that one day she would have to tell Travis. It was his right to know. Now he would search Potter out of revenge, and she did not want that. Granger understood and told her that when he found Potter that he would pay. Della quietly said, "I know."

Stewart Granger left Della a much humbled man. Nellie watched him leave and came into the parlor to talk to Della. Della sat back in her chair and started sobbing. Nellie ran quickly to her side and wrapped her arms around her. When Della came up for air, Nellie handed her a napkin. Nellie asked if Granger had upset her, to which she said no. They had come to an understanding. Nellie just got to the point and asked her what was wrong. Della took Nellie by the hand and repeated everything she had just confided in Granger. Nellie now was the one who was sobbing her heart out! Both women held each other for a long time. Both women were going to be okay.

Stewart Granger left Coyote Springs with a sense of justice. He was the one who had hired Potter, and he was going to find him. He felt tortured learning what Potter had done to Della. No man should ever lay a hand on a woman, much less tie her up like a wild animal. Granger felt sick again, which made him want to find Potter even more. Granger was in deep thought when Travis was riding toward him. Both men reined up. Travis asked him what his business was at Coyote Springs. Granger said that he paid Della a visit to apologize for all the pain he caused her.

Travis looked at Granger and saw that he was being honest, and he wanted to know how Della reacted. Granger told him that they both said what needed to be said and that she forgave him. Granger told Travis that he was going to make Potter pay. Travis just looked at him and said, "You are going to have to stand in line."

Stewart Granger looked at Travis and told him that after all he had done that he had no right to tell him what to do, but he told

Travis to leave Potter alone. Granger went on to say, "If you love Della, you need to be with her and keep her safe. Do not do what I did and lose the one thing that matters most in your life." Granger told Travis to marry Della and do not look back. Travis told him that he would marry Della, but the time was not right. Granger told him, "Time has nothing to do with it. Follow your heart."

Travis told Granger that he understood, but Potter was under his skin, and he wanted him out of their lives forever. Granger looked at Travis and asked him how he would feel if they worked together to find Potter. Granger went on to say that they both want the same thing and have Della's welfare in mind. Travis held his hand out, and Granger took it in agreement. Travis asked Granger if he would follow him to the mine to meet a few more men who would help in their search. Granger said, "Lead on."

Silas Reed was surprised to see Stewart Granger ride up alongside Travis. He knew something was up from the way the two were talking. Travis introduced the two men and went on to say that they had combined forces to find Potter. Silas said that was the best news he had heard all day. Soon the men were in deep discussion on their next move.

Della felt like she had a weight taken off her. She had not told Travis yet, but she would once Potter was captured again. Nellie felt better also. She had a feeling that Potter had been up to no good. If she had a chance to get hold of him, he would not get away!

Cal Potter had left his hideout to take a better look at his surroundings and make sure of all his options before he made his move. He needed to be able to escape without being noticed. Potter remembered the trails around Coyote Springs. He had ridden them often. That was how he found his hideout. It was near where Della would take her evening walks. He had always stayed in the shadows so he would not be noticed. He was double-checking other places that he would watch from when he heard voices. He stopped and moved in closer, daring to get close enough to see who it was. Potter was taken aback when he saw two men, even more surprised to see Granger and Travis acting like old friends. This just made the game more interesting indeed. They were working together.

C HAPTER 5

Potter listened for a while then made his way back to his hideout, and by morning, he was going to put his plan into action. He did not choose this spot for nothing. Soon he was making his way to the hilltop that overlooks Coyote Springs. He lay flat and blended into the brush. He could not take the chance of being seen. Potter made his way to this spot over the next several days, waiting for the chance that he was waiting for, and it would be very soon.

Coyote Springs was always busy; everyone was starting to relax, and the fear of Cal Potter was far away. There had been no news about Potter. Some thought he was long gone. Della was feeling happier and not worrying as much. Granger came often for supper or just to visit; his friendship was growing with Travis. Della noticed the friendship and knew it was a good thing. Forgiveness is good.

Granger and Travis had searched all over and at times had come close to Potter. If the men had been alone, they would have been dead. They had been that close to Potter. Potter was keeping track of the comings and goings around Coyote Springs. Granger and Travis had slowed their tracking of Potter, for both men were getting frustrated. Yet both men had a feeling that he was close by. They would have to be more watchful.

Coyote Springs kept Jim West, Doc's driver, busy. He would make several trips a day. He was on his way back to town after delivering a couple of boarders. He was waiting for Nellie to bring a couple of plates for him and Doc's supper. He was anxious to get to town. He finally started out of the gates, going at a far trot, when he saw something lying across the road. He thought that it was odd and slowed up the team. He had just come to a stop and slowly got out of the rig to go and move the limb. He had just bent down to pick up the end of the limb when he was hit from behind, and all went black.

Della had walked onto the porch to water some plants. Nellie was in the kitchen finishing supper for the boarders. Della looked up and saw a buggy heading her way. She laughed that Jim had forgotten his usual supper from Nellie. She started down the steps, going toward the buggy, as Jim was turning the buggy to head out. Della came up to Jim and asked him what he had forgotten. When Della looked up and saw him, her face went ashen, and she turned to run, but it was too late! Della felt her body being pulled into the buggy, and it started to move. She tried to scream, but hands were covering her mouth. She fainted.

Time had gone by; Nellie had started serving supper to the boarders in the main dining room, then she would serve the family in the smaller dining room. She noticed that she had not seen Della since Jim had dropped off the two boarders. Nellie went to the porch. She knew Della was watering the plants, but there was no Della. Nellie started to worry; she hurried down the steps to the barn but still no sign of Della. About that time, Sam and Travis were riding through the gates. Nellie came running out of the barn toward them, screaming that Della was gone, that she had vanished! Travis's heart went cold!

Travis asked Nellie when was the last time that she saw her. Nellie said it was earlier when Jim had dropped off new boarders, got his supper, and left. Travis told Sam to go and tell Silas and ride out to let Granger know he was going to town to catch up with Jim. Both men rode out in a cloud of dust. Nellie was wringing her apron with tears running down her cheeks. All she was thinking was that Potter had gotten Della!

Travis headed toward town and came to a dead stop. He saw a figure on the side of the road. It was Jim, and he was in bad shape. Travis was able to get the injured man on his horse and headed back to Coyote Springs. Nellie was on the porch about to go in when she saw Travis riding in hard. She shaded her eyes and saw that he had someone on the horse. Travis reined up. She saw that it was Jim. She gave a shout to a couple of the men at the barn to come help. Nellie told Travis to go and tell Sheriff Tom and to get Doc to come out. She would take care of Jim. The men took Jim in with Nellie close behind.

Travis turned his horse and rode as fast as he could to town. He pulled up in front of the jail in a cloud of dust and ran in. Travis was out of breath, and the sheriff told him to settle down and to tell him what was going on. Travis took a deep breath and told him that Della was missing and that Jim had a gash on the back of his head. Travis said, "I know that Potter is behind this!" He told the sheriff that he had to go tell Doc.

Doc had met Travis at the door, for Doc had seen him ride in hard. Travis told him what happened. He told Doc that Jim was in a bad way. Travis was still in a rage, and Doc took hold of his arm and told him to get ahold of himself. He had to get a leveled head on him and concentrate on Della. Doc went on to say that Potter is out for blood this time, and it is not Della's. Travis calmed down some. He agreed with Doc. He went to help Doc hitch up his buggy and get himself a fresh mount. Both men headed out of town as fast as they could go.

Sam had made it to the mine and gave the news to Silas before heading to the Triple S. Silas was worried and knew the time had come. He told Autumn what had happened and to gather her things to go and stay with Nellie until this was all over. Autumn went and gathered her things and was soon headed to see Nellie. Silas hollered at Sparrow and told him to get the others ready. Sparrow was gone in a flash.

Sam rode his horse as fast as he could to the Triple S. He was met at the gate by Cheekman, who followed him up to the house. Granger saw the men approach from his front window and came out onto the porch. Sam got off his horse and caught his breath. He told Granger that Della was missing and that Potter may have her. Granger clinched his fist; Sam went on to say that Jim West was hit on the back of the head but will make it. Sam said that Della had been gone for hours and could be anywhere. Granger told Cheekman to let the men know and that at first light they would start a search.

He told Sam to let Travis know that at first light to be ready. Sam nodded and left.

Travis and Doc made it to Coyote Springs to find that Autumn was there. She told Travis that his pa had sent her to stay awhile. He was relieved and glad she was there. Doc went to find Nellie who took him to see Jim. He had a deep gash on the back of his head. Nellie had hot water and bandages ready, Doc soon had Jim resting as he stitched up the gash. Nellie kept the bandages coming, and Autumn put a salve over the wound. Soon, Jim was resting comfortably. Doc and the women came out on the porch to get some air.

Doc hated to see his friend in such pain, and knowing that Della was in Potter's clutches again, it worried him even more. Travis asked about Jim. Doc said he would need several days of rest, and then he would see. The gash had been deep, and Doc was worried that some damage may have been done. Nellie and Autumn had worried looks on their faces. Both women were in deep thought.

Della awoke, feeling sore, coming to her senses, remembering that she had been kidnapped by Cal Potter. She tried to get up but found that she was chained to a post. She heard a sound and turned toward it. There sat her captor with a smile on his face, relishing every minute of her pain. Potter was calculating his next move; he had his prize now. What to do with it? This time, he was not going to lose.

Potter sneered at Della and said, "Well, look at the little saloon girl now. Oh, I forgot that was who you used to be. Now you are a lady, a very wealthy lady at that." Della cringed. She knew she was in trouble, and there was no way out of it this time. Potter was rambling on, not making any sense. She decided to stay quiet and speak only when he asked her to. He was laughing how he left poor Jim on the side of the road to die with a big gash on his head. Della said a silent prayer that Jim would be all right. Potter got up to retrieve something and came back with a plate, the one Nellie had fixed for Jim. He ate it in front of her, and soon he was asleep by the fire.

Della was too scared to be thirsty or hungry. She was looking for a way out. She could not make out where she was. It was dark, and the campfire was a poor light. She hoped by morning she would be able to find out where she was. She had to be strong, so she tried to sleep somehow, knowing that come morning, it would be no different.

Travis had walked down to the barn, looking up to the hill where he used to watch over Della. He was thinking about where she could be. They had searched everywhere, and still no sign of Potter. Now with Della gone, he was helpless. He was not going to get much sleep that night. In fact, there were few who could sleep.

Come morning, Travis left early to meet up with Granger and the Triple S hands. They were going to retrace their steps and look harder. Silas put the mine on hold so that he and his men could help in the search.

Nellie, with the help of Autumn, was trying to carry on with the running of Coyote Springs. The boarders were all concerned about Della and hoped she would be found soon. Nellie would smile and thank them, but behind her smile, she was falling apart. Autumn sensed that Nellie was in pain and asked if she could help. Nellie started crying, and soon everything came spilling out. Nellie was sobbing so hard. Autumn was shocked and concerned for Della. Nellie told Autumn to swear not to tell Travis. Autumn patted her hand and told her not to worry. Della was in trouble, and Travis needed to know how serious the situation was. Nellie agreed. Autumn told Nellie she would tell her son what he needed to know.

Autumn left Nellie to look for Travis. Nellie tried to pull herself together, but all she could do was cry. Sam had taken over Jim's duties for the time being, and he saw how this was getting to Nellie. He gave her a hug and told her that he loved her and that all would be well in the end. This made Nellie feel somewhat better, and she gave him a hug. Nellie said, "We survived the last time, and we will survive this time." Sam left her with a smile.

Autumn had made good time catching up with Travis as she came upon the group of men. Travis reined up when he saw his mother coming. He knew something was wrong. Travis and Granger rode to meet her. She slowed her pace as they met under an oak tree. Travis was quick to ask what was wrong. She said that she needed to tell him that there was something he needed to know about Della.

Autumn looked past Travis to Granger and said, "Your friend has something to tell you." Travis asked what she was talking about. She rode her horse up beside her son and placed her hand over his heart. She looked into his eyes and told him that it was time for him to heal and to come full circle to accept what he would hear and do the right thing about it. Autumn turned to Granger and said, "You have both traveled the same path, and one of you will have to learn from it as the other already has." She turned and left.

Travis turned to Granger and asked again what she was talking about. Granger said, "Step off your horse, and I will tell you what Della confided with me on the day I had visited her." Travis got down with a look of puzzlement on his face. Granger had told his men to carry on the search and that they would catch up later.

Granger sat on a log as Travis did the same. Granger began speaking and did not stop until he had told Travis everything that was spoken between him and Della. When Granger had finished, Travis had a face that you could not read. He waited for Travis to absorb what he just told him. When Travis spoke, he was shaky at first, then his voice got stronger. He wanted to know why Della did not tell him. Granger told him, "She was about to, then Potter escaped. She was afraid you would hunt him down for revenge, and that is not what she wants." Travis said she was right, but he understood now.

Travis told Granger that he would not stoop to Potter's level. He knows that he must do the right thing and settle the score once and for all. Granger told him that they both had a score to settle, but only one would go through it. Travis told Granger he did not understand what he meant. Granger said, "What has been done we cannot change. What Della went through is something she never should have, and it was both our faults. Mine because I hired Potter and yours because of a love lost to him. Do you want to lose again? If you call Potter out, you will lose Della anyway you look at it. Someone will die in the end. I have lived through my hell and have come to terms with what I have done. Potter will pay."

Travis's mind was reeling. He had a grudge for Potter for so long that he was scared to show Della how much he really loved her. He was afraid that Potter would destroy her. Yet her love was so strong, it endured the torture that Potter had put her through. Travis turned to Granger and said, "Potter is all yours. I am going to find Della." Granger smiled, and soon the two rode off to catch up with the Triple S hands.

Travis was feeling better. He had a purpose now, and there was no turning back. The guilt he felt all these years was gone. He was going to find Della and marry her. Whatever happens to Potter will not be on his hands. He was done with the man. Travis looked at Granger and knew that Granger had to do what was to be done not only for himself, but also for Della, for Gracie, and yes, for his Julia.

C HAPTER 6

Della woke up feeling stiff. Her hands were tied behind her, with a chain wrapped around her right foot. Her whole body was numb. She knew she was not going anywhere. She looked around and found herself in a room with dirt walls of sort. On the fire was a pot of coffee and a skillet of biscuits. Her stomach rumbled, but she tried to hide the fact that she was. She saw Potter coming from her right side to the fire. He stooped down to pour himself a cup of coffee and sat back on his haunches as he sipped it. He soon turned his head to look at Della, and he got up to stand over her.

Della tried to be calm, but she was unsure of what he could do. Potter stood for a moment then turned back to the fire. He was not saying a word. Della was tired, and she fell unconscious. Potter turned and looked at her again. He knew he would wear her down, and this time, he would finish what he had started the last time. Time passed, and Della awoke again and found that her hands were untied, and she was lying on a thin blanket. She tried to sit up but did not have the strength to.

Potter walked over and set a plate in front of her that had a biscuit and a cup of coffee. She slowly reached for the biscuit and ate it slowly and sipped on the coffee. Potter was saying how much he had missed her. Della shrank at his words. He came over to sit next to her as he stroked her hair. He was saying that they had had a lot of good times together. Della almost choked on the coffee; Potter got up laughing.

Potter left Della for what seemed a long time. She was able to stand some and look around more. She could not figure out where she was. She could not hear any sounds; it was not a house of sorts, then she thought a cave.

If she was in a cave, then she must be near Coyote Springs. She backed down when she heard Potter coming in. He had changed clothes, and he set a box next to her where he put a jug of water, a cup, and a tin of biscuits. When he had done this, he turned and walked back the way he came. Della thought this was strange but knew that he was leaving her for a time. Now she was worried.

Travis and Granger had searched over half the day, so they decided to go to Coyote Springs for lunch and any news. When they approached, they saw Sheriff Tom on the porch. The sheriff greeted them both and told them that he had some news of sorts. Both men got off their horses. Sheriff Tom told the men that he had gotten a telegram from Louisiana that the Smiths, Bob and Polly, had been murdered in one of the hotels in New Orleans.

Granger said, "That sure sounds like Potter tying up loose ends." The sheriff agreed. Travis said that they looked all over, and there was no sign of Potter or Della. It was like they fell off the face of the earth. The men were not getting anywhere. Nellie came out and told the men to come in for some dinner. Autumn was coming out of the kitchen when she caught Travis's eyes. She knew he was going to be all right, and she smiled. Soon the table was full of men eating and talking, mostly trying to figure out where to look next. Travis slipped out to go for a walk and clear his head.

He walked down to the barn and leaned on the fence; he was remembering the day Della had walked down the same path to get him for supper. He had his shirt off. She had seen his scars. He had sensed that she had wanted to ask him how he got them. He had put his shirt back on, avoiding any questions. Her eyes were so green in the moonlight. He had wanted to kiss her, but again, he pushed her away. He remembered all the times that he had pushed her away, especially the last time. He knew that he had broken her heart. Travis hit the fence with his fists. He was only trying to protect her, and this time, he really messed up!

Travis heard his name being called from up at the house. Granger and Sheriff Tom had come out on the porch to look for Travis. It was Granger who Travis had heard calling him. Travis walked up as Granger was about to get on his horse. Granger said he was heading back to the ranch and would be back at first light. Sheriff Tom said he had to go, too, and best of luck to both. Travis shook their hands and told them he would see them tomorrow. Soon he was alone on the porch. He walked to the edge of the porch and looked up on the hill, thinking hard on where they could be.

Della had been trying to free herself from the chain that was around her foot. She would take only small sips of water for fear that Potter may not come back. The post was old, so Della tried to push it back and forth to see if it would move. Her efforts were working, but she tired easily. She worked with the post off and on. She looked at the chain around her ankle. She thought that if she took off her shoes and stockings that the chain may slip off. She tried it, but it did not work. She got back up and looked at the post, then she saw the nail that was driven to hold the chain. She looked around to see if there was anything to help pull the nail out, then she saw the plate and the cup, both made of metal. She had hope.

Cal Potter had slipped out, leaving Della by herself. He had business to take care of, and by the time he got back, Della would be ready for what he had planned. He had a gun that had been hidden by the Smiths. They had done such a great job helping him that he hated he had to kill them. Yet he swore that this time around, he was not going to mess up and take what was his!

Della soon gave up on the post and lay down to rest. She had a feeling that Potter was up to something. She told herself to be strong. She tried to think of positive things, but her thoughts would stray. It was dark, and there would be no fire, no light for her to see by. She stared into the darkness. Yet she kept saying, "You must be strong!"

Nellie had been beside herself and could not do anything but cry. She was angry with herself and mad at the world. She lit into Travis several times to the point where he stayed away from her altogether. Sam tried his best to calm his wife, but she was inconsolable. Autumn sat with Nellie and would comfort her by holding her hand or just lending an ear. Autumn told Nellie that she needed to get a grip on herself for Della. She said, "Think of what Della has gone through and survived. No telling what she is being put through as we speak." Nellie stopped crying and dried her tears. She looked at Autumn and told her she was right. Nellie said that she was being so selfish and not strong like Della. She told Autumn that things were about to change and that she would be stronger and fight.

Cal Potter had slipped through and made his way to New Orleans. He figured that he would be safe there and would blend in well. He had friends that helped him along the way. He was unaware that "wanted" posters were in the area. He shrugged it off when he saw one. He was not going to be around that long, just needed to pick up a document and head back to Texas.

Potter had employed a certain clerk to make up any documents that he may need. He had the clerk to have him a marriage license prepared, completely notarized, ready for signatures. Potter was pleased with the document and paid the clerk. He was in a hurry to get back to Texas to his bride. He was laughing as he walked out of the office. People stopped and looked at him for a moment before walking on. Potter felt like he was in control.

Potter had checked into a charming hotel for the night. He figured a good bath, supper, and a good night's sleep would be good before he got back to the cave. He had also splurged on a new suit of clothes. He also had to figure out his next move once Della signed the document, then he would decide on what to do with her. Then he smiled. Della could stay right where she was at Coyote Springs in a cave until she died, a perfect burial plot. Potter smiled again.

Potter came downstairs to have his supper; he had asked for a table in the corner away from prying eyes. He had ordered a steak and a bottle of wine earlier; it was being brought out as he walked across the room to his table. A pair of eyes was watching him as he walked by and never left him. He was unaware that he had been noticed. The eyes were the color of hazel and were shaded by a veil that draped off her hat. She sat for a few moments before reaching into her purse for the paper she had inside. A slight glance of the paper, she put it back and finished her meal and was soon gone.

Della's supper was water and dry bread. She could not hear any noise. It was quiet, way too quiet. She was wondering if Potter was coming back, or was this the end for her? She wept and tried to sleep again. She had to keep trying the post. She was not giving up.

Sheriff Tom, Travis, and Granger continued their search with no luck. Sheriff Tom told the men that the time had come to stop looking. Travis shook his head but knew he was right. Granger agreed because he had to. None of the men wanted to stop, but they knew they were running out of options.

Travis headed back to Coyote Springs to break the news to Nellie and Sam, Nellie was going to be upset. Sheriff Tom headed back to town with a heavy heart. He hoped that he would hear something soon from his "wanted" posters. All everyone could do now was to wait.

Doc was in his office when the stagecoach arrived. A woman was stepping down from the coach. Doc got up from his chair for a better look. She was an exceptionally beautiful woman and was traveling alone. She picked up her bag and made her way over to the Rosewood Inn. She moved quickly as if she did not want anyone to see her. Doc went back to his desk and to his business. The woman had made it to the inn and went inside.

Rachel Sanders was at the desk as the woman approached, asking for a room near the front if possible. Mrs. Sanders said that she had a nice room. The woman said her name was Jill Cane and would like the room for a week if possible. Mrs. Sanders laughed and said, "If you had come a week or so ago, there would have been no rooms". Jill Cane asked why. Mrs. Sanders went on about the trial of Cal Potter and how he escaped and now had kidnapped Della Butterfield.

Hank Sanders came into the room about then, and Rachel asked her husband to take the bags up for Jill Cane to her room. Jill followed Hank up the stairs to a nice bright room. Jill went to the window and looked out; the town had not changed much. Mr. Sanders asked her if she needed anything else. Jill told him no, and he was soon gone. Jill went over to the bed and sat on it and took off her hat. She doubted herself but knew in her heart she had to try again. She had to be sure what she heard was true. How she prayed.

Travis was walking in a daze. He felt helpless. He could not get Della's face out of his mind. If only he had let go a long time ago. He did not like himself at all. He knew he had to find Della and hoped that it was not too late. Travis was not giving up. He knew Potter would show his hand and soon.

Della was trying to keep her eyes focused. She heard a noise and soon made out the outline of a figure. Potter had returned. She shrank back into herself, unsure of what he was going to do. He came to squat in front of her and stared for a moment. He rose and went to a low table and lit a lamp.

Potter reached into his coat and pulled out a piece of paper and looked at Della. He went to her and reached for a key in his pocket to unlock the chain around her foot, then helped her to her feet. She was unsteady as Potter dragged her over to the table and made her sit down. He put the paper in front of her and told her to sign it. Della tried to read it, then she saw what it was. She said no and was backhanded for her outburst.

Potter was losing his patience with Della; he grabbed her by the arm and put the pen in her hand. Della still tried to resist. He hit her again, making her fall out of the chair. Potter stood over her, telling her that it was no use. He wanted to finish what he started. He told her that she was not going to make it out alive, no matter how much she resisted. Della slowly got up with the help of Potter back into the chair. Della had a calmness about her as she picked up the pen and signed her name. Potter snatched it out of her hands and put it back into his coat pocket without glancing at the page.

Potter grabbed Della by the arm and threw her back on the pallet on the floor. He put the chain back on her foot and stood up. He looked at Della. He turned away and walked over to blow out the lamp. There was total darkness. Potter was laughing as he left Della, and the sound grew fainter until he was gone. Della was alone.

Potter had made sure no one would be able to find Della. He had what he wanted, and she would not be around to say otherwise. Potter was feeling very sure of himself and decided to visit an old friend he had scores to settle with, and there was no turning back.

Della lay in the dark, knowing that she had to try to escape. She could not give up, especially to a man like Potter. Not after what he put her through. She knew he was not coming back, at least not for a while, for he was after Travis and Granger. She had time to work on the post. She was going to survive!

Potter decided that he would save Travis for last. He wanted Travis to find Della in the cave and chain him to her dead corpse. He laughed again. He headed his horse on along until he heard voices. Potter forgot how close he was to the gold mine. He touched his pocket and smiled. He slowly rode past, making little sound. Time was on his side, and he was going to enjoy every minute of it. He had sat in that jail cell thinking about his every move. He was free and was going to stay that way.

C HAPTER 7

Jill Cane had settled into her room and came down for supper that evening. She ate in silence and soon retired to her room. She sat by the window in her room in deep thought, asking herself if this was the right thing to do. She needed answers. She had left Rosewood so long ago with a heart that was broken. She loved a man with all her heart, yet he changed in front of her to a bitter, spiteful man. He was so wrapped up in trying to have everything in sight that he lost the one thing that mattered most. Jill sighed. Maybe it was a hopeless cause, yet from the news that she heard, she had hope.

She was going to lie low for a while longer and see what she could learn. She was tired and soon went to bed. She was thinking about the man she saw in New Orleans; he was up to no good. She hoped that she was not too late as she lay thinking of days past. She remembered when she first came to Rosewood, how young she was, a bride with a whole new life in front of her. She was in love. He was tall and dark, a man who knew what he wanted and took it.

Time passed, and their love was tested in many ways, leading up to when she had no choice but to leave him. He had become a stranger to her. She felt that he loved material things more than her. She left without a word. He went into a fit of rage and became a madman. He told everyone that she had run off with a whiskey peddler, not wanting everyone to know the truth. She went away but not far so that she could keep track of him, for her love was still strong. She turned over and finally went to sleep. Tomorrow was a new day.

Nellie was sitting on the porch, looking up to the ridge as she did every evening since Della was kidnapped. Nellie was sick with worry, wondering where she was. Nellie blamed Travis for not being a man and marrying Della after the mess Potter and Granger had put her through. She had confronted Travis and told him a thing or two. Deep down, she knew that Travis loved Della and tried his best. Just to find her would help ease their minds. It was driving everyone crazy. Everyone blamed themselves one way or the other. One thing for sure, Potter had the upper hand for now, and she was praying that he had not hurt Della.

Silas was worried, too; he saw the torment that Travis was going through. He knew that Travis would do the right thing, but deep down, what was the right thing? Granger had come to his senses and was trying to make amends for the harm he had caused. There had been too much pain, and it was not over yet. Silas walked to the mine, looked around. He shook his head and headed toward his home.

Granger was confused like everyone else. They had ridden all over the county and had seen no sign of Potter. Even the "wanted" posters brought no results. He was pacing as usual in his living room and stopped in front of the fireplace. On the mantel, he saw the smiling face of his Julia. He picked up the picture and touched her face with his finger lingering for a moment, then placed it back on the mantel. He heaved a heavy sigh and was lost in thought.

Della was in and out of sleep. She would try to work the post by moving it back and forth. It was a slow process, but it was moving. She had hope. She tried using the tin cup on the nail. She worked on it until she was tired. This had become her routine. It was her life, and she would not give up. Della was going to make it, and she had to get out before Potter found out what she had done. He would certainly kill her! The thought made her work more.

Travis had moved out of the house and was staying up in a loft in the barn. He was able to lie on his bed and look out at the hillside and think. He was trying to think where to look next and hoping that Della was okay but, most of all, if she still loved him. He soon turned over and was in a fitful sleep as he did every night.

Potter had made his way to the Triple S. He waited to make sure all was clear as he made his way up to the house. He slipped in the shadows up to the front window and saw Granger standing in front of the fireplace in deep thought. Potter made his way around to the back of the house and slipped into the door of the kitchen. The house was semi dark as Potter made his way toward the living room; Granger was turning from the fireplace when he saw Potter come into the room with his gun drawn.

Granger looked at Potter and told him that he had been expecting him. Potter grinned and told Granger to drop his gun. Granger undid his holster and laid it on the floor as Potter was walking toward him. Potter bent down to pick it up without leaving his eyes off Granger. Granger asked Potter, "Where is Della?" Potter just laughed and said, "That little problem had been taken care of." Granger flinched at Potter's words, hoping that no harm had come to her. He did not press the matter. Potter told him to have a seat and not to move. Potter walked around and blew out all the lamps and drew the curtains closed. He was making sure that no one knew he was there.

Granger was watching every move that Potter made. He could tell that Potter was uneasy, and he had every right to be. Granger had hoped Potter would show. Potter had just turned away from the window when footsteps were heard on the porch. Potter turned to Granger. He knew he was about to be caught. He fired his gun, missing Granger by inches, for Granger had already hit the floor, drawing a gun from under the chair, firing a shot as Potter went through the doorway.

The front door was busted open by several hands just in time to see the back side of Potter leaving out the back of the house. Granger came out of the living room, telling his hands to spread out and find Potter. Granger thought he may have winged Potter; he had made a clean getaway. Granger came back into the house and saw a drop of blood on the floor. He followed the drops all the way back to the living room. Granger smiled. He had not missed.

Potter was riding for his life. He was mad at himself for falling into a trap and getting shot by Granger. Potter could hear riders coming his way. He could not go back to the cave. He had to hold up and tend to his arm. He took an old trail that was overgrown and came upon a house. He rode around back and saw that it was abandoned.

There was a shed where he put his horse. He made his way to the house and pushed his way through the front door. As he entered, he fell to the floor, passing out completely.

Some of the hands returned and said that they lost track of Potter. Granger told them that they will head out at first light. Granger told them that he had wounded Potter but was not sure how bad he was. Granger had been lucky that night, but he was more worried about Della, if she was alive or not, but most of all, where she was.

Potter awoke feeling very weak and sore. He had barely made it through the door of the house. He slowly raised himself up to lean against the wall. He had been shot in his right shoulder and lost a lot of blood. He finally made it to his feet to search for something to bandage his shoulder. He used an old tablecloth; he was still weak but made his way around the house. He found some whiskey in the parlor that he soon finished off. He fell asleep on a couch.

Potter awoke feeling some better but hungry. He got his wits about him and looked around the house. He went upstairs to find a lot of dust and spiderwebs; he went into one of the rooms and saw it had belonged to a woman. He found a dressing table and saw a picture and was surprised to see Della looking back at him. He was taken aback for a moment, knowing that could not be right. He looked more closely then remembered Granger's wife, Julia. Potter looked around and knew he was in the house of Stewart Granger, where he had lived with Julia.

Potter went back downstairs on out to where he had put his horse. He went to his saddlebags and got some jerky. He knew that he could not stay there much longer. Granger would have his men out searching for him. He was in a pickle for sure. Potter got on his horse and slipped into the woods; he would stay off the trails and slip past those who were looking for him.

Potter could hear the thunder of horse's hoofs in the distance and knew that it was Granger headed to get Travis and fill him in on the news. Potter winced in his saddle. He had ridden a short distance and had to stop to rest. He needed his shoulder mended.

Potter made his way to the side of Coyote Springs and saw Granger with his men riding through the gates. He could see Travis come out of the barn to meet them. He had turned and went back into the barn, coming out with his horse. Potter saw another man heading to the barn and figured it was Sam. He also joined the men, and the group rode out. Potter smiled and made his way down the hill; he went around back to the kitchen and slowly came up to the window of the kitchen to peer in. Nellie was busy in the kitchen. Potter slipped through the back door. He went behind her as she turned. She screamed and dropped the dish that was in her hands to the floor.

Potter put his gun to her face and told her to be quiet, very quiet. Nellie was shaking so hard, but she did as she was told. Potter asked her if there was anyone else in the house besides the boarders. She hesitated but said no. He instructed her to get whatever she may need to tend to a gunshot wound. As she turned to go to the cupboard, he told her to bring whiskey too. Nellie grabbed a basket and began putting what she needed in it. He was watching her closely, so she had to be careful. Potter pointed his gun at Nellie and told her to head to the barn to saddle her horse. He walked close beside his horse as they made their way to the barn. Nellie was being calm. She was hoping that someone would ride in. He told her to mount up, and he tied her hands to the saddle horn and took the reins of her horse. He led her out the way he came in.

Nellie looked back, glad that Autumn had been on an errand. No telling what would have happened to her. She thought about her Sam and that she may never see him again. Potter jerked the reins of her horse to make it go faster. He was feeling weaker and needed to get out of sight and quick. Potter took the trail that led to Granger's old home. He told Nellie to get down and put the horses in the shed. He took her by the arm and led her into the back door of the house. He untied her hands and told her to look at his arm. Nellie looked around and got the woodstove going and put a kettle of water on.

Nellie tore open his sleeve up to his shoulder; the bullet was still in his shoulder. She told him that she would have to get the bullet out and would have to use a knife. He looked at Nellie and told her not to try anything, that is, if she ever wanted to see Della again. Nellie stopped for a moment and started to clean the wound. She asked for his knife, which he slowly handed to her. Nellie took the knife and told him it was going to hurt a bit. She set to work.

Nellie had brought a bottle of whiskey, which she used to pour over the wound. Potter winced and grabbed the bottle to take a long drink. Potter had to keep his wits about him. Nellie dug into the wound to get the bullet out. She sewed the wound and then put a salve over the stitches, then the clean bandages. Potter was light-headed, but he was still in control and took Nellie by the arms and put her in a storeroom. He locked the door and pushed a cabinet against the door so she could not get out. Potter finished the rest of the whiskey and went back to the couch in the front room. Getting shot was not part of his plans.

Jill Cane rented a buggy for the day from the livery stable. She had Hank Sanders rent it for her. He had brought the buggy to the hotel where he helped her into the buggy and told her to have a nice drive. Jill smiled and flicked the reins for the horse to go. She was soon headed east out of town. Jill was on a mission and hoped that she would find her answers. She drove along for a while and soon was passing Coyote Springs and saw a group of men that she figured were looking for Cal Potter. She was thinking of the Bagwells. Tom and Alice had owned the place. It seemed so long ago. Jill knew where she was going because it had been a while since she had been there. Would it be the same?

Della was unsure if it was night or day. She was trying to keep her mind clear, but it was getting hard to do. She continued to work on the post, and making progress seemed like an eternity. She sipped her water slowly, making it last. Her biscuits were hard, but she was able to eat them. Della knew that Potter had left her to die, and it was up to her to get out of this mess, for no one would be able to find her.

Jill found the road she needed to take but could barely make it out. It was overgrown and had become a trail for a horse much less a buggy. Jill made it through and went into a clearing where she reined up the horse. She sat to look around. Jill stepped down, taking it all in with memories flooding her mind. He had kept the house. She was surprised yet hopeful, thinking that he may still care. Jill took the steps of the porch slowly, still looking around. She went up to the door to open it, finding it unlocked, and she went in.

Jill walked into the foyer, seeing all the furniture and everything just as she had left it. She went toward the parlor to see that it all looked the same too. Jill was about to step further in when she saw a figure lying on the couch, Cal Potter. She took a small step back, trying not to make a sound and was turning to leave when a voice behind her said, "Where are you going?" Jill froze.

CHAPTER 8

Travis, along with Granger and his men, had just finished a wide sweep and still had no sign of Potter. Granger swore that he had shot him. The men turned to head back to Coyote Springs. Autumn had gone into town for some supplies since Sam was riding with the men. She reined up at the house just as the men were coming through the gate. Travis trotted up to help. Sam followed. Autumn said that she would go in and help Nellie to bring out some refreshments.

The men were bringing the groceries into the house, heading to the kitchen. Autumn was coming out of the kitchen with a look of concern on her face. They asked her what was wrong. She said that Nellie was not there and that there were broken dishes on the floor in the kitchen. Both men searched the house. No one had seen her since breakfast and were starting to wonder about lunch.

Sam went to the porch and told Granger that Nellie was missing. They heard Travis holler round back. The men hurried around to where Travis was squatted, pointing at blood. Travis said, "Potter has been here." Sam took off running to the barn to find Nellie's horse gone. He slumped on a bale of hay.

Autumn was in the kitchen and saw the cupboard door opened. She looked inside and saw that Nellie's basket of medicine supplies was gone and a bottle of whiskey. She also noticed something else and smiled. "Good thinking, Nellie."

Jill Cane knew she was in trouble. She had no idea that Potter had come back to Texas, yet here he was. Potter was looking at her as if he were seeing someone else. He was still weak from his gunshot and whiskey. He needed more sleep. He took Jill by the arm and led her to the kitchen, where he moved the cabinet away from the storeroom door. He unlocked it. Nellie had heard him and was standing up when he opened the door and shoved a woman at her. He slammed the door, locked it, and put the cabinet back in front of the door. They could hear him swearing as he was going back to the parlor. He had another problem and was bleeding again. He needed rest. He finished off the whiskey and threw the bottle into the fireplace.

Nellie turned to help the woman to her feet. As she was getting up, Nellie was taken aback when she looked at her face. Nellie gasped and said, "Oh my! It cannot be!" The woman dusted off her clothes and said, "Yes, it is me. Julia Granger." Nellie stood for a moment, then she reached and gave Julia a bear hug. Julia laughed for a moment and returned the hug. Nellie took a deep breath and told Julia what was going on and that they were in danger.

Julia had found a box to sit on while Nellie was telling her about what had happened since she had been gone. Julia was amazed and shocked at what she had learned. Nellie caught her breath and sat down beside Julia. She took Julia by the hand and told her that Stewart always loved her and still did. Julia's heart skipped a beat. She was right in coming back. She turned to Nellie and told her, "We have to get out of here." Nellie agreed!

Travis, Sam, and Granger had ridden day and night looking for Della and now Nellie. The men were worn out. Silas had ridden up to Coyote Springs to let them know that they had not seen or heard anything either. Autumn came out to the porch and called the men in to eat. Travis looked like a broken man as he went up the steps. After they had all eaten, it was decided that everyone should go home and get some rest. They would start back come morning. Silas gave his wife a kiss and a hug and told her to be careful. Autumn said she would.

Della was awake again. Her eyes had gotten adjusted to the darkness. She could see a faint light in the distance. Her bread and water were about gone. She had the post loose enough to pull it out of its hole. Della was weak but was not going to let Potter win. She paused when she heard a noise that sounded like scratching. The sound was getting closer. She stopped and turned toward the sound; she was looking into the face of a coyote.

The coyote had been curious. The male had been hunting and picked up a scent that he knew. He had followed the scent deep into the cave until he stopped and found what he was searching for. He stepped to the side of Della, watching her. Della saw that he was not afraid. She reached for a biscuit and broke off a piece. She gently tossed it to the coyote. He stepped for an instant, then he slowly went toward the bread. He sniffed and soon gobbled it up. He sat and looked at Della for what seemed a long while, then he turned and went back the way he came. Della felt hope. Somehow, the coyote was a sign. Della went back to work on the post.

Potter had slept all night and awoke stiff and sore, his shoulder hurting. The bandage needed changing. He had to let Nellie out to do it. Now he had two women to worry about. He would deal with Granger's wife. Killing her would be easy. He stood and went to the kitchen. Potter had a rough time moving the cabinet. He was weak but managed. He unlocked the door and told the women to open it and come out one at a time.

As they came out of the storeroom, Potter pointed his gun at Julia and told Nellie that he needed his bandage changed, and if she tried anything, he would kill Julia. Nellie told him to find a seat and to put away the gun. Potter made Julia sit across from him and not move. Nellie added wood to the stove to get the water hot to clean his wound. Nellie washed the wound then put more salve on it before wrapping a fresh bandage around it. He put his shirt back on and told the women to get back in the storeroom, and he locked the door.

Hank Sanders had come downstairs, searching for Jill Cane. He had rented her a buggy for a morning ride the day before, and he had not seen her return. He saw Rebecca, his wife, at the counter and asked if Jill Cane had returned from her buggy ride. Rebecca said that she had not. Hank went across the street to the livery to see Doc. Doc saw him coming and went to greet him. Hank told him that he was concerned because Jill Cane had rented a buggy and had not returned. Doc told him that he was about to see him about this matter too. He told Hank not to worry. He would go and let Sheriff Tom know of the missing woman.

Doc stood and watched Hank go back to the hotel. He turned and closed his office door and headed over to the sheriff's office. Sheriff Tom was pouring a cup of coffee as Doc walked in. Doc told him to pour him one too. Sheriff Tom handed a cup to Doc and asked him what got him out so early. Doc told him that Hank Sanders had rented a buggy the day before for one of their guests, a Jill Cane, and she had not returned.

Sheriff Tom was short on sleep like most men in the county. No leads on Della or Nellie, much less Potter. Now Doc was saying another woman is missing. The sheriff said he would talk to Hank and get a description of the woman. Both men finished their coffee in silence. They were up against a wall and nowhere to go. Doc broke silence by saying that Potter would slip up. Sheriff Tom told him it better be soon. Time was running out.

Sheriff Tom went to see Hank after Doc left. Hank and Rebecca said that Jill Cane was a striking woman, dark haired, young, and beautiful. They told him that they thought she may have been to Rosewood before because she knew so much about the town. The sheriff told them that he would inform everyone to be on the lookout. Sheriff Tom decided to ride out and see Travis.

Travis had a fitful night. He tossed and turned. He had a dream or a nightmare. He could not get it out of his mind. All he remembered was Della lying on a dirty mat. Alive or dead, he did not know. Travis started doing chores around Coyote Springs. The livestock had to be fed, as some fence mending. Sam was still working in Jim's place. He was on the mend. Autumn made sure that Jim got plenty of fresh air. Autumn took over for Nellie. Life was going on but so different.

Sheriff Tom was riding in the gate and hollered at Travis, who looked up from his work and waved. Sheriff Tom reined up at the porch and told Jim hello and that he was looking good. Jim told him that he should be back at work next week. Autumn was coming out the door with a tray of coffee for the men. She set it on the table and left. Travis came up the steps and asked the sheriff why he was out so early. Sheriff Tom was pouring the coffee and said that one of Hank Sanders's boarders has come up missing, a woman, Jill Cane. Travis took the cup from the sheriff and said that he had not seen anyone here lately. Sam just shook his head and asked if Potter could be involved. The sheriff shrugged his shoulders and said, "Your guess is as good as mine. We are all at our wit's end." The men agreed and finished their coffee. Sam said he had to be going. Jim told him, "Hold up, you are not going anywhere. I am back to my job. Sam, you need to be here, and no one is talking me out of it!"

Jim stood up and walked down the steps. He shook Sam's hand. He stepped up into the buggy and was off in a cloud of dust. He was back to what he loved doing. He also wanted to help find Potter. Sheriff Tom left the two men on the porch also. Sam picked up the tray and went inside. Travis stood up and looked up to the ridge. He saw a small figure, but realized it was a coyote. The coyote had been sitting there all morning, waiting. Travis saw that the coyote was not moving as if to say something. He remembered the many evenings sitting on the porch with Della listening to the coyotes play. He looked back again, and the coyote was gone, on the hunt again.

Nellie and Julia were planning on their escape. They were locked in a storeroom. The women knew that Potter would be on the move soon, and they would be extra baggage. Potter was thinking the same thing. He looked out the front window and saw the buggy that Julia had ridden up in. He was in a panic! He had to get rid of the rig somehow. He went out and unharnessed the horse and let it go. He knew the horse would go back to the stables. He pulled the buggy into the woods and covered it the best he could. Potter was feeling woozy and headed back into the house. It was time for him to move on, and he was going alone.

Nellie and Julia had been busy in the storeroom. They found some rotten boards in the back wall and were working to remove them. They heard Potter coming, so they put the boards back against the wall and moved in front of them. They were surprised when he did not open the door. The women stopped and listened. Potter was gathering up the provisions and getting ready to leave. He was leaving the women locked in the storeroom. As Potter took the coffeepot from the stove, he started to laugh in an evil way. The women heard the laugh. It chilled them to the bone.

Cal Potter had a plan on how to get rid of the women and get back at Stewart Granger. Granger would pay dearly this time. Potter stoked up the fire in the stove until he had a nice fire going. He took a stick of wood and got it nice and hot; he went from room to room, setting the house on fire, then he went out the front door, throwing the stick back into the doorway, and walked away laughing. Potter got up on his horse and grabbed the reins of Nellie's horse and headed out. He needed to be far away and fast.

Nellie and Julia smelled smoke and knew they were in trouble! They worked nonstop to pull the boards from the back of the storeroom wall. The house was blazing hot and fast. Stewart Granger happened to be out at the corral when he saw smoke on the horizon. He knew where it was coming from.

Granger hollered at Cheekman, his foreman, to saddle his horse and get the men together. Soon the men were riding fast as they could. The women were working fast but were losing ground. The smoke was intense and making it hard to breathe. They had gotten a couple of boards loose, but something was blocking their escape. Julia went down. She had passed out from the smoke. Nellie rushed to her side, trying to get her up.

Granger and the men rode up as the house that he had built for his Julia was in full flames. There was nothing the men could do. Granger's heart was heavy. He got off his horse and started to the side of the house near the kitchen. All he could do was watch it burn. Nellie was trying her best to push her way through the wall. She was making progress when a ball of fire came through the ceiling. She grabbed Julia and let out a bloodcurdling scream!

Granger froze and went toward the scream. Cheekman was close behind. Granger saw boards on the back of the house partially moved, then he saw movement. He dove in and grabbed an arm. It was Nellie. Granger helped Nellie to get clear out of the house. Nellie screamed and said, "There is someone else in there." Granger thought it was Della and headed in. He scooped up a limp body of a woman and made it out just in time when the ceiling fell through.

Granger staggered toward Nellie and Cheekman and dropped to his knees, carefully laying the woman in his arms down. Cheekman brought blankets from his saddle and water. They wrapped Nellie in one of the blankets and gave her some water. Granger was given a blanket, and as he was putting it on the woman he just saved, he froze. It could not be! He wrapped her gently as he pulled her close to him and sat on the ground, holding on for dear life, with tears streaming down his face. A hand reached up and wiped a tear. Julia was home.

C HAPTER 9

They watched the house burn to the ground, Granger still holding Julia. Nellie felt a sense of relief and was glad to be alive. Cheekman brought his boss out of his trance and told him that it may be a good idea to get the women home. Granger said, "Yes, let us go home." Granger got up and helped Julia to her feet. Cheekman had found the buggy in the trees and hitched up his horse to it. Granger helped the women up, and soon they were taking Nellie to Coyote Springs.

Travis had seen the smoke way off on the horizon. He went back to his work before he headed out to search again. He saw the coyote again in the same place as before. It would turn his head to look back from time to time. Travis thought it was odd but remembered what his mother had taught him. She told him to always open his heart and mind to nature and learn from them to survive. He thought that he would see what the coyote was up to when he saw a buggy and several men coming through the gates.

Travis started hollering for Sam, for he saw who it was. Sam came running out of the barn. Both men headed to the house. Nellie almost jumped out of the buggy into Sam's arms. Granger helped Julia down and led her up the steps. Granger went on to tell the men what had happened. Autumn came out and ran to Nellie and gave her a big hug! She then took the women inside to tend to their burns and let them freshen up.

Granger had gotten the women to Coyote Springs safely. Autumn came out and said that Julia was asking for him. He excused himself and went to her. She was in the parlor resting but stood and came to him when he walked in. Nellie slipped out to go to her Sam.

56

They did not even know she was there. Julia went to Granger's arms, and he held her close. Then he bent and kissed her long and hard. Yes, Julia was home, and this time for good!

Nellie went to the porch to see her Sam, who hugged her until she could not breathe. She was glad to be home. Granger and Julia came out and joined them. Nellie told them that Potter had kidnapped her to take care of his shoulder. Granger said, "I knew I hit him." Nellie said, "You did, but not well enough." Nellie had asked him about Della. He just gave her that cold stare. Nellie said she was locked in the storeroom every night. Julia spoke up and said that she had just gotten into town and had checked in as Jill Cane. She took Granger by the hand and said that she wanted to see if the home he had built for her was still there. Julia said that she had gotten Hank Sanders to rent it for her. She knew that Doc would have recognized her.

Julia went on to say that when she walked into the house, she was surprised by Potter who was lying on the couch. He threw her in the storeroom with Nellie. Julia said that before she had left New Orleans to come to Rosewood, she had seen Potter there. Travis perked up and asked her how long ago that was. Julia told him about a week. Travis was wondering what he was doing in New Orleans. Did he take Della there? Granger spoke up and said that Potter had connections in Louisiana, more so in the New Orleans area.

Nellie said that she had done something that was wrong of her but, considering who it was, had to do it. Nellie looked at Autumn as she said that she had added a special salve to his wound every time she cleaned it. Nellie went on to say that she had added some poison to the salve. Autumn said, "I thought so. When I looked in the cupboard after you were taken, I saw my tin missing, I knew it was a sign." Nellie smiled and nodded. Everyone was looking at each other, and all said that she did the right thing.

Granger stood up and told them he was taking Julia home and that he would have Cheekman return the buggy to Doc. He also said that Cheekman would tell Sheriff Tom everything. Travis was thinking about New Orleans as they left. He would have to do some digging on Potter himself. Autumn brought him out of his thoughts and told him that she was going home. She was not needed anymore. Travis gave his mother a hug, and Nellie did also and told her, "Thank you." Autumn told Nellie that she was a strong woman and that she learns well. Travis took his mother to the side and told her about the strange behavior of the coyote. Autumn looked at her son and asked, "What does your heart say?" Travis said, "Follow it." Autumn smiled.

Cal Potter had gotten out of the area in the nick of time. He saw the smoke and knew that he had taken care of Nellie and Julia. The shot had put a big dent in his plans. He would have to go back to the cave and make sure that Della was dead. If she was not, then he would put her out of her misery.

Silas saw Autumn coming up the road and went to meet her. She got down from her horse and hugged her husband, telling him she was home; Nellie had been found and was safe. Silas told her that they had seen and smelled smoke. Autumn said that Potter had tried to kill Nellie and Julia Granger. He set fire to Granger's house, leaving the women inside. Granger and his men saved them just in time.

Cheekman had returned the buggy to Doc, who followed him over to the sheriff's office. Cheekman told them that they had rescued Nellie and Julia Granger from a burning house. Potter tried to kill them both. Doc said, "Hold on, Julia Granger? I thought it was Jill Cane." Cheekman went on to say that she had used a fake name, for she did not want anyone to know she was in town. Sheriff Tom asked about Della. Cheekman shook his head. "No news."

Nellie was glad to be back home. She kept busy and pushed the last few days out of her mind. Nellie went to the back door where she always put out scraps and added a few more. She had seen the tracks and knew the coyotes were getting fat. She smiled and went back inside. She looked out the window as she did dishes and caught a glimpse of something going by. She went to look out the back door window, hoping to see a coyote enjoying his meal. She saw him come up very cautiously and choose only a bone with meat on it. He did not stay and eat it, yet ran off with it. Nellie went back to her work, thinking at least they were eating.

Della had gotten the post out of the ground. She was very tired and had no strength to move anymore. She heard the scratching sound again and saw her friend watching her. He approached her to the side and dropped something on the pallet beside her. Della was amazed how the coyote knew; she gobbled down the meat hungrily. He turned and was gone.

Her friend came often throughout the day, bringing her food. She was able to gain some strength to move closer toward the entrance of the cave. She had to keep her wits about her. She would talk to the coyote so she would not lose her mind. He would sit and listen to her; he seemed to try to keep her moving. Della understood and followed him, it was a slow process, but she was going to succeed.

Jim had brought Doc out for a visit to see Nellie and Sam. Nellie was pleased to see them and that she was glad that Jim was better. Nellie had another good cry. Doc told her that everyone was being positive as possible that Della would be home soon. Nellie wiped her tears.

Travis rode into Coyote Springs just as Doc and Jim were leaving. He had met them at the gate and had a few words. Travis went to the barn to put his horse in a stall. He soon walked up to the house and to the kitchen. Nellie turned as he came in and set a plate on the table where he was about to sit. She sat across from him and touched his hand; she told him that she was sorry for being so cross with her and that she hoped he would forgive her. Travis patted her hand and said that he already had. Travis looked up at Nellie and said, "I am going to find her." Nellie told him, "Yes, I know you will."

Chapter **10**

Cal Potter had backtracked to where he had Della hidden. He wanted to see her for the last time. Call it a moment of weakness, but he knew Della was a strong woman. He reined up in front of the entrance of the cave. He moved brush and boards so he could hide his horse inside. Della froze. She heard the rustling noise just ahead of her. She struggled to move faster to get out of sight. She heard a horse neigh and a voice cursing. Potter was back.

Potter lit a lantern and crept in at a slow pace; he was not feeling too well. He had broken into a sweat. He figured he had a fever and needed to rest. He had to take care of Della first. As he continued into the cave, his lamp lighting his path, Della could see him as he walked past her. She had made it to another section of the cave thanks to the coyote.

Della knew she had to be ready because he would soon learn she was gone. Potter arrived where he had Della chained, and as his lamp lit up to show where she was, she was gone! Potter went mad. He was swearing and searching all around. He could not figure out where she was. The entrance had not been disturbed. Then he saw that the post was gone. He knew that she had freed herself and was close by.

Della heard him screaming like a madman. The coyote had returned, and Della saw he had friends. The coyote stood in front of her as if to protect her from Potter. Potter was feeling worse by the minute. He was swearing and was trying to search for Della. He knew she was nearby somewhere. As he came around the corner, his lamplight showed eyes looking at him and low growls. He was sweating so bad that his eyesight was blurred, and he was stumbling. He took a step toward the eyes and saw that it was coyotes. As he drew his gun from his holster, he stumbled and fell to the ground, hitting his head on a rock and knocking him out.

The coyotes circled him. Della inched her way to his lifeless body; she searched in his pockets and found the key to her freedom. Della was finally free of the post. She retrieved the lamp and adjusted her eyes so she could find the gun. She smiled in a devious way as she took the chain off her foot. She had all the strength in the world as she chained Cal Potter to the post that he had left her chained to die.

The coyotes moved toward the entrance to lead Della out. Her eyes were slowly getting adjusted to the daylight. She breathed the fresh air into her lungs. She was alive and free!

Travis had finished his meal and left Nellie to her work. She was humming as he left. Travis headed to the porch and looked up on the hill, and there was the coyote. Travis looked again and saw several, then suddenly like on cue, they began to howl and yip. Nellie came running out of the kitchen, and Sam came out from the barn wondering what was going on. The coyotes were making a lot of noise. Travis told Nellie and Sam that he was going to check it out. As he stepped off the last porch step, Nellie screamed and said, "Look, coming through the gates. It is Della!"

Travis was running as fast as he could with Nellie and Sam right behind him. They reached Della as she started to fall off the horse, Travis caught her, and both fell to the ground. Nellie was kneeling beside them, crying, "Oh, Della, my Della!" Della raised her arm and pointed toward the hilltop. The coyotes were still making noise. All she said was "Potter" and passed out.

Travis picked her up with Nellie close behind, taking her to the house. Travis was hollering at Sam to saddle their horses. Once Della was safe inside the house, Sam had the horses ready at the porch. Travis jumped up, and soon they were off. Nellie was in a state of joy taking care of Della. She looked bad, so worn out, and dirty. Nellie gave her a bath and put a nightgown on her. She had washed her hair, all this as Della was sleeping. Nellie went to the kitchen to prepare soup for when she woke up and plenty of water. She was so sick and thin.

Potter had come to and heard the coyotes as they howled. They were blocking the entrance, so he could not leave. Potter tried to get up but felt something heavy on his foot. He reached down to see what it was and touched a chain. He had been chained to the post. He went crazy and cussed a blue streak. He looked for his pistol but could not find it. He was still feeling sick. The coyotes had stopped howling. He thought, *Good, they are gone.* He was going to get out as soon as he could stand, then he heard voices.

Travis and Sam had just ridden up. That was why the coyotes had left. Both men got off their horses and drew their guns, walking cautiously into the cave. Once inside, they were taken aback at the sight they saw, Cal Potter chained to a post. Potter looked up at Travis and swore like a madman. Travis turned and told Sam to fetch his pa and his men and bring a wagon. Sam turned to leave and hesitated. Travis told him that he would not do anything to Potter. Someone else already has. Sam left.

Silas saw Sam riding up fast and told Silas that Della was home safe and that Travis needed him and his men to haul Potter to jail. Silas hollered at Autumn, who soon headed to see Della. The men followed Sam to where Travis and Potter were.

Silas shook his head at the sight of Potter. Travis stepped back and let the men load him in the wagon. Travis told them to take him on into town, he was going to see Della and to tell Doc to come running. They left with Potter cursing in the back.

Travis headed back to Coyote Springs to find his mother helping Nellie with Della. He told them that he had sent for Doc. He also told them what they found up on the hilltop. The coyotes had Potter trapped in a cave, the one that he had Della hid in. Funny thing was he was chained to a post. Nellie stood up and walked to the end of Della's bed and raised the covers. She told Travis to look. Della's ankle was red and swollen with marks of being restrained. Travis turned away.

Travis went to sit in the chair that Nellie was sitting in by Della. He stroked her hair and whispered his love to her. Della moved; Travis knew she would come back to him. Autumn came into the room with Doc. Doc was worried about Della's condition and asked

Travis to leave. Travis did not want to go but did. Sam was in the hall, and the men went to the kitchen for coffee.

Doc had Nellie and Autumn stay. He had to examine Della and see if she had any injuries that needed attention. He saw that the women already had things under control and told them so. Doc checked her ankle, and it was wrapped nicely. He was thinking that Potter was a cruel man. He told Nellie to make sure Della regained her strength by eating and drinking plenty of fluids. He told her that she would have to make Della drink until she got strong enough to do so herself.

Silas and the men had dropped Potter off to Sheriff Tom, who was surprised and very pleased to have him in his cell again. Deputy Banks was also; he was not going to fall for his tricks any longer. Potter was out of it. He had been bleeding from his gunshot wound and was dirty. Doc was out at Coyote Springs, so the sheriff and deputy cleaned him up and redid his bandage. Doc would have to look at it when he got back. Potter was in no hurry.

Chapter 11

Sheriff Tom had sent word to Judge Cartwright that Cal Potter was caught, and that Della Butterfield was safe. The judge was relieved to hear the news. He sat back in his chair and thought about the lives lost and gained. Life was funny sometimes. Potter would not be leaving his jail cell anytime soon. He took up pen and paper to send word to both lawyers of Potter's arrest. Joshua Wetherspoon, when he got word, cringed inside.

News had reached the Triple S that Della had been found and Potter was in jail. Stewart and Julia both were relieved. They had been rebuilding their relationship since the house fire. They were given a second chance and were happy. Stewart sighed and looked at Julia. She knew he felt responsible for bringing Potter to Rosewood. Julia took him by the hand and told him to forgive himself, for everyone else already had. He put his other hand over hers and said he would.

Cal Potter woke up some better and looked around. He was so out of it, he could not remember a thing. He could not believe his eyes! He slowly sat up on the cot and swung his legs to the floor. He let out a line of words that no one would want to hear. Potter caught himself when he heard movement outside the cell. He lay back on his cot to gather his thoughts. Sheriff Tom was heading out the door to get some air when he heard all the commotion. He had to smile to himself as he closed the door behind him.

Potter was furious that he got caught. He had to think hard what to do next. He flinched as he turned over in his cot. He closed his eyes and smiled. Potter's plan was already in play. He had the marriage certificate that Della had signed all tucked away. He sat up suddenly, thinking about when he woke up at the cave he had been chained to a post, just like the one he had chained Della to. Who did that? Where was Della? Did she? His memory was foggy, but he knew he had to complete his mission.

Deputy Eli never told the sheriff how he let his guard down and had let the mystery visitor see Potter. He had heard Potter ranting and raving. He was not going to lose his job and make that mistake again. Besides, his head still hurt from the bump he got when he escaped.

Della was in and out of consciousness, but knew she was home and safe. Nellie sat with her during the day and Travis all night. Autumn would give them a break when they needed it. Travis was torn watching Della struggle. He had to get some air. He felt he was in the way. Travis walked to the porch where Nellie was watering the plants. She looked up and saw that he was troubled. He told Nellie that he was going for a ride to clear his head. He stood for a moment and took a deep breath, then he headed to the barn. Nellie soon saw him ride off. She paused and wondered where he was going.

Sheriff Tom had sent another telegram to the judge. He told him that Potter was sick and that Della was in a bad way. The judge replied to keep him posted on Della's condition. He said nothing about Potter.

Potter was on the mend slowly, biding his time. Deputy Eli was keeping a closer watch on him. Potter knew this and waited.

Nellie kept Della as comfortable as possible. She would talk to her to hang on and fight, not let the likes of Potter beat her now. Della was in and out but was fighting hard. She grew stronger and steadily worked at it. She had asked for Travis several times; Nellie finally told her that he took a ride and had not come back. Della was thinking why and where did he go. Nellie bit her lip and told her that he had been gone for several days. Della had tears in her eyes.

Della seemed to change overnight. She had gotten strong enough to sit up and eat her meals. She did not say much, still in some pain. Nellie and Autumn took turns in getting her up to walk. She soon was on her own. Della was a fighter; her thoughts went to Travis. Had he deserted her? She had walked out onto the porch and looked up to the hilltop and saw her friend. In silence, she thanked him for saving her. She made a promise to herself that she would deal with the days ahead and do what she needed to do. She turned and walked back to her room and slept.

Della awoke early the next morning and had gotten dressed herself. She surprised everyone when she came into the kitchen to sit at the table. Nellie brought her some coffee and breakfast. Della ate and made small talk; Nellie knew that she was better. Della got back into her old routine with some changes. She would go behind the barn every evening and practice her shooting. Sam was concerned, but Nellie knew she was getting ready to do something.

Della aimed her pistol and fired. She emptied her gun, dead on the target. She was not going to let Potter or anyone get the best of her again. Della was taking a stand.

Sheriff Tom came out for a visit one afternoon to check on Della. He saw firsthand that she was going to be okay. She saw him ride up and walked him up to the house. Nellie was coming out of the house when she saw them. She turned to go back in. Della walked up the stairs with a pistol strapped to her, the sheriff close behind. Della asked him to have a seat, as Nellie brought out some coffee on a tray. Sheriff Tom said that he wanted to talk with her. Nellie excused herself.

Della knew that it was time to tell what had happened. She poured their coffee and started telling the sheriff what had all happened. By the time she had finished talking, the sheriff leaned in to her and said, "You mean to tell me you chained Potter to his own post?" Della nodded yes. Sheriff Tom told her that she was the bravest woman he has ever met. Della shook her head and said, "No, I wanted to kill him on the spot." She went on and said, "That would have just made me like him, a small-minded cruel person with no regard for any human dignity or life."

Della told the sheriff before he left that she was ready for the trial. He agreed and rode off with a much greater respect for her. When the sheriff got back to town, he went to send another telegram to the judge, saying that whenever date he wanted to set for the trial that Della was ready. Sheriff Tom left and went back to his office to see Doc walking up. Doc said that he would see Potter's wound if he did not mind. The sheriff said, "Come on in."

Potter heard the men as they came through the door. He moaned and rolled over in his bunk. Doc gave the sheriff a look as he lifted the keys off the peg. Sheriff Tom told Potter that Doc was here to see him. Potter muttered, "It is about time." He was feeling worse. Doc walked into the cell and told Potter to lie still and let him take a look. Sheriff Tom leaned against the cell door and watched. Doc started unwrapping the bandage and saw that the wound was not healing. In fact, it was getting worse. Doc sat back and reached into his bag to retrieve something to clean the stitches with. He also gave Potter a couple of pills to take to help him with the fever and pain. Doc put a new bandage on and got up to leave. He told Potter to rest and that he would check on him tomorrow.

Doc turned to Sheriff Tom and told him that Potter was good enough to stand trial. Potter jumped up from his cot, which forced Doc to run out the cell door. Sheriff Tom drew his gun and told Potter to settle down as he locked the cell door. Potter was still screaming as the sheriff closed the main door to the cells.

The scream was quieted down some. Doc turned to the sheriff and told him that Potter may make it to the trial. Sheriff Tom stopped and asked Doc what he meant. Doc told him that when Potter had kidnapped Nellie to help him with his wounded shoulder, she had helped him all right. She had used a salve that she put poison in. The sheriff let out a soft whistle. Doc went on to say that it is slowly killing him, and he turned to leave.

Sheriff Tom watched him walk out the door. He would keep this to himself. He was the law, yet under the circumstances, he did not blame Nellie at all nor Della for wanting to kill the man. He hoped that Potter would live to be tried and punished. In fact, he is already being punished.

Sheriff Tom knew that this time around, security had to be better than the last time. He had to hire more deputies and make sure all exits and Potter were well guarded. He knew that Potter would try something again and that he would be ready for it this time.

Potter was still hopping mad, but he came to his senses. He sat on his cot, trying to wrap his mind around on what to do next. Time was drawing close. He had his ace in the hole. When to play it, time would tell. He was feeling all fuzzy in his head. Must be the pills that Doc gave him. He lay back on his cot and slept.

CHAPTER 12

Travis had left to clear his head, but he kept riding, lost in deep thought. He stopped when he was tired and ate when he was hungry. Everything was a blur. Travis kept going until he could go no more. He stopped in a secluded area and stayed to clear his mind and his heart.

Della, in the meantime, was taking care of herself and Coyote Springs. Since Travis had left, she had to hire extra help. She had hired Randy Crow and Andy Marsh. She also hired a new cook, Nancy Robertson, and gave Nellie her freedom to do what she wanted to do. Nellie was not too happy at first, but she came around. She took Nancy under her wing and showed her the ropes. Nancy was a quick learner.

Sam got smart too. He had let Billy Wilkes run the store and live upstairs. Billy was the son of Chester Wilkes, line foreman for Stewart Granger. Billy stood by Sam and worked hard for him, Sam thought of him as a son. Nellie and Sam would be able to concentrate on finishing their home and enjoying each other.

Autumn had gone home soon after Della was back on her feet. She was disappointed in her son taking off when Della needed him the most. She told Silas that Travis had taken off. He told her not to worry, that he would be back. Autumn told him she had a bad feeling and was worried. Silas just gave her a hug. She sighed, hoping she was wrong.

Silas kept the mine going. He had Sparrow and the other men to board up the cave where Potter kept Della prisoner. He kept constant watch over Coyote Springs and those who lived there. He shook his head thinking about his son and what had gotten into him. He did not tell Autumn that he was worried too.

Della rode into town once a week to make a deposit from the gold mine. Silas had Sparrow drive Della and Bo Jackson; Dan Fields would ride as guards. The weekly visits were never the same. Robert Sessions looked forward to these visits. His bank was doing very well. He had learned his lesson well after his past dealings with Stewart Granger and Cal Potter. His wife, Annabelle, had led him in the right direction too.

Della took advantage of her trips to town to visit Ms. Nancy. Sometimes Doc would join them and catch up on the news. Doc said that Rosewood was booming thanks to Coyote Springs. Della laughed. Ms. Nancy said that she would be glad when the trial came and gone. Della smiled and said that she was more than ready. Doc had wanted to ask about Travis but thought otherwise.

Potter was watching from his cell window, seeing her come and go. He was furious inside! To think all that gold was his, not hers! He hollered at the sheriff that he wanted to see his lawyer. Sheriff Tom told him that he would get word to him. He sent the deputy to send the telegram to Joshua Wetherspoon.

Potter lay back on his cot with one arm behind his head. The other one still hurt. He was in deep thought on how he was going to use his lawyer, and he knew that he had to watch the deputy. Potter went back to the window to see Della leaving town. He clinched the bars of his cell. Della would pay this time. He would not hesitate.

Travis had left in a hurry and did not bring any provisions. He had to go into the nearby town of Dry Fork. He rode into town as the sun was going down. He pulled up to the dry goods that was still open and walked in. The shopkeeper looked up from the counter and asked him if he needed any help.

Travis made a striking figure in the doorway. He had not bathed or shaved in a while. Travis said, "Yes. I need a few items." He handed the clerk a list. There was movement behind Travis. He jumped. He had been on edge for a long time. A vase dropped and shattered to the floor. Travis drew his gun and fired toward the sound. A woman screamed. Travis turned cold.

Travis came to himself and realized what he had done. The door flew open, and the town sheriff came in, gun drawn on Travis. The clerk told the sheriff about the vase being dropped and had startled the man that he fired. Luckily, Travis had missed. Out from behind a shelf, a woman appeared. She hastily told the sheriff that it was her fault. She went on to say how sorry she was. The sheriff relaxed and told Travis that he better be more careful the next time. Travis said he would pay for all the damage. The clerk said that would be fine and that he would not file charges.

Travis paid for his items and the damages. He tipped his hat and apologized to the woman and the clerk. She smiled and accepted. She turned and walked out of the store. Travis gathered up his purchases and followed her out. The woman kept walking down the street, never looking back.

Travis packed his horse. Soon Travis was heading out of town in a fast trot. A crowd had gathered outside the store and watched him ride off. A man leaning against a post lit a cigarette and flicked the match into the street. A woman came up beside him and whispered in his ear. Soon the man was on a horse following Travis. The woman smiled and drifted back into the shadows.

Travis kept riding, cursing himself all the way. He let his guard down. He needed to get his head together. The sooner, the better. He had too much on his mind to know that he was being followed.

Now the woman had made her way to a back stairway where she made her way upstairs to a small room and lit an oil lamp. She turned toward the closet and opened the door; she was soon packing a bag and was heading back out the door. She made her way to the stable and rode out of town at a slow pace.

Potter had an early morning visitor, his lawyer Wetherspoon, who had arrived the night before. He had stayed at the Rosewood Inn. Sheriff Tom said that he could have a private conversation with his lawyer but would remain locked in his cell. He brought a chair for the lawyer and left them alone. Sheriff Tom stepped outside and sat in a chair to read the daily news. There was only one way out, and it was the front door.

Lawyer Wetherspoon leaned in to tell Potter that the trial was a lost cause, and he felt he could not represent him. Potter leaned into the lawyer, grabbed him by the neck, and told him that he was going to do what he was told. Potter flung the lawyer back into his chair and told him to sit if he valued his life! He fixed his glasses and composed himself, then asked Potter what he wanted him to do. The lawyer knew that Potter was an evil man and knew where he lived and would hurt his family. Potter got close to the lawyer and proceeded to tell him what he wanted done.

Sheriff Tom folded his paper as Wetherspoon came out the door. He told the sheriff that he would be staying in town until the trial. He said he would be in and out to visit his client. Sheriff Tom told him, "That would be fine." The lawyer walked away wiping his brow. He was in a lot of trouble and had to think.

Potter smiled despite himself; he lay back on his cot, waiting for his lunch. Deputy Eli was coming up the walk with Potter's lunch. He saw that the man did not look so happy. Sheriff Tom opened the door for him. I food smelled good. Both were suddenly hungry.

A woman rode into town as the sheriff and deputy went in to eat their lunch. She reined up in front of the Rosewood Inn. She stepped off her horse and dusted herself off. She saw a sign in the window that a cook was needed, so she went in to apply. Rachel Sanders had needed a cook and had just put it in the window. She was pleased that she got results so fast. The young woman introduced herself as Sally Anderson and that she had just gotten into town looking for a fresh start. Rachel shook her hand and asked if she had cooked before. She said, "Yes, and I have references." Rachel told her that she would try her. She told her that the job came with a room. Sally smiled and said, "That would be simply great." Rachel said, "Let us get you settled in, and start as soon as you can." Sally told Rachel that she had to take care of her horse. Rachel told her that she would get her room ready and sent her to Doc at the livery stable.

Sally went outside, smiling to herself as she walked her horse over to the livery. Jim West met her at the gate. She introduced herself and told him she was the new cook for the Rosewood Inn. She needed to have her horse stabled. Jim took the reins and told her he would take care of her horse. Sally thanked him and turned to leave.

Potter was in his normal position looking out the window of his cell, feeling sure of himself. He saw the woman ride into town and then go to the livery. He just shrugged his shoulder and went to lie on his cot. Lunch was good. Wonder what was for supper.

Sally Anderson had settled into her room; she went downstairs to see Rachel in the kitchen. She looked around and liked what she saw. She loved to cook and would show Rachel what she could do. Rachel had taken an instant liking to this girl; she did not talk much and knew what she was doing. Soon, Sally was on her own, with Rachel checking in from time to time.

The Grangers, Stewart and Julia, had come into town. They had been like two lovebirds since the accident. They came into Rosewood for supper. Rachel seated them at their favorite table. Stewart ordered a bottle of wine and took a rose from the vase that was on the table and gave it to Julia. She took it with so much love in her eyes. They chatted and enjoyed their meal.

Attorney Wetherspoon came in as the Grangers were leaving. He went to sit at a far table. He was lost in thought. He felt someone watching him. He looked up and saw a young lady smiling at him from the kitchen doorway. He returned the smile. He ordered his dinner and ate in silence.

Travis finally settled down for the night. He fed his horse and stoked the fire. He kept thinking about what he had done, shook his head, and settled down in his blanket. He looked up toward the stars and sighed. Then he heard a coyote call. He shivered.

A figure was standing behind a lone pine, watching Travis turn in for the night. He knew he would have to make his move and soon. He stepped back, got on his horse, and faded into the night.

C HAPTER 13

Judge Cartwright had gotten the wire from Sheriff Tom from Rosewood. He leaned back in his chair and reread the wire. He lowered the paper and looked out the window in deep thought. He slowly turned toward his desk and called his secretary in. He told her he would be going to Rosewood for a few days and to cancel all his appointments. He grabbed his coat and hurried out the door.

The judge wanted this trial tI over as soon as possible. The last one did not turn out too well, and people got hurt. He would talk over with the sheriff to do things differently this time. He had been busy since he had gotten back from Rosewood the last time. He ate an early supper, packed, and went straight to bed. He wanted to get an early start come morning.

The rider had ridden back into Dry Fork. He made his way up a stairway up to a dark room. He opened the door, closed it behind him, and went straight to bed to sleep.

Sally had put in a full day and finally went to her room. She was pleased about how things had turned out. She hoped that she would be able to do her job and do it the right way. Soon she was fast asleep, anticipating what the next few days would bring.

Sheriff Tom was up early making his rounds. He had heard that Rachel had hired a new cook, so he headed over to see Rachel. He wanted to check out the new cook. Deputy Eli was walking up, and the sheriff told him he was getting breakfast this morning. The deputy told him he would have the coffee ready.

Sally had been up for hours, it seemed; she was busy with the breakfast crowd. Rachel told her to make three meals for the sheriff.

He would pick them up or send someone else to do so. Sally told her she would have them ready; she stopped a moment as Rachel left the room. She turned and completed her task.

Sheriff Tom had come in and was talking to Rachel. He asked about the new cook and how it was working out. Rachel told him that she was a jewel and was doing a wonderful job. She said, "When you taste her cooking, you will agree." Sheriff Tom told her that she may be taking a chance by hiring a stranger. Rachel put her hands on her hips and said she liked the woman and felt no problem at all. She told him to stop fussing. She left him, returned with the basket of food, and handed it to him. Sheriff Tom was at a loss for words and just said, "Thank you," and headed for the door, leaving Rachel with her hands on her hips.

Sheriff Tom ran into Potter's lawyer as he was going out. Wetherspoon held the door open as the sheriff walked out. He did not speak much and went on in to have his breakfast. The sheriff continued his way, smelling breakfast every step he took.

Potter was up looking out the window as usual, his favorite pastime. He saw breakfast coming. His stomach churned. He was not fully well yet. He could just get his arm healed fast enough.

Deputy Eli had made coffee and opened the door for the sheriff and soon all was quiet, enjoying breakfast. Sheriff Tom took another bite, and he stopped and thought, *Well, she could cook.*

Travis woke up feeling sore all over. Sleeping on the ground was no picnic. He started thinking what he was doing. He stirred up the coals and started a fire, adding a pot for coffee. He managed to fry up some bacon and opened some hard biscuits to warm in a pan. He leaned back and sipped his coffee and took a bite of biscuit. His thoughts went to Della.

He was scared and had failed as a man. Everything had happened so fast; he never got a chance to ask her to marry him. He felt trapped. He loved her, but he doubted himself, never felt good enough. He had let her down time spnd time again, and now he left her when she needed him the most. He hit his fist on the ground, wiped his brow, and poured another cup of coffee.

He could not protect Della no matter how hard he tried. She was the strong one. She had escaped from Potter all by herself. She did not need him. He told himself it was time to move on. He would tell her he never loved her. Potter had gotten the best of him. He was a beaten man. He threw his coffee into the fire and started packing up. He would go into Dry Fork and send Della a telegram. He could not face her, not now, not ever.

The man turned over in his bed and put his feet to the floor. He made his way to the washbasin and poured water into the bowl. He washed and shaved, then changed into clean clothes. He headed to the door and soon was going down the stairs. He walked over to the hotel to grab a bite of breakfast; he had been thinking about what to do and what to do next.

Travis made his way into the town of Dry Fork, his mind in turmoil on the telegram he was about to send. In his heart, he felt it was the right thing to do. He would head up to the Rockies and get lost in the world. He reined up in front of the telegram office and dismountedI tied his horse and walked in. The man behind the desk greeted him. Travis said, "I would like to send a telegram."

Across the street at the hotel, the man having breakfast watched Travis as he came into town. He wiped his mouth with a napkin and laid his money for breakfast on the table. He put his hat on as he walked across the street to the telegraph office and waited outside.

Travis was having a tough time writing down what he wanted to say. He scratched through the words and started again. He became so frustrated that he would wad up the paper and throw it in the wastebasket and start again. He finally finished and handed it to the clerk and paid the man. With a heavy heart, he turned and left. Travis did not see the man leaning against the wall as he walked out. He just took the reins, jumped on his horse, and headed out of town. He was never coming back.

The man watched him as he rode off before he went into the telegraph office. He inquired to the man behind the desk if the gentleman who just left sent a telegram or not. The man said he did after several attempts to write it down. He sure went through the paper. The man went to the wastebasket and took out one of the papers that

Travis had thrown away. He opened it and read it. The man asked for a fresh sheet of paper and began to write. He gave the paper to the clerk and paid him. He headed in the direction that Travis had gone. The man was hell-bent on catching up with him.

Sheriff Tom finished off his breakfast and told his deputy he was going to make his rounds. Potter was quiet for now; he sure slept a lot. He stood and stretched, grabbed his hat, and went out into the street. He stopped and looked around Rosewood. Before he could take a step, he heard someone shouting. He turned to look toward where the sound was coming from and saw that it was Red Grover from the telegraph office. He was also the postmaster. Sheriff Tom asked him what in the world was he shouting for. Red said, "I just got a couple of telegrams from Dry Fork. One for you and the other for Ms. Della." He went on to say that he had just missed Jim to take it out to her.

The sheriff told Red that he would be more than glad to take it to her. He always enjoyed his visits, and now he had an excuse to have another. He glanced at the telegram and thought Dry Fork, wondering what it was about. He went back inside and told his deputy that he had to go to Coyote Springs to deliver a telegram to Della and that he would be back shortly.

Sheriff Tom opened his telegram and read what was in it. He slowly looked up and folded the telegram and put it in his pocket. He went to the stable to get his horse, dreading this visit.

Della was taking each day as it came, she was dreading the trial, but this time, she knew it would be all over soon. She was feeling much stronger and had kept up with her shooting. She was becoming more independent and surer of herself. Her heart was on the mend. She kept busy and was not lingering on Travis. He had shown how he felt by leaving her when she needed him the most.

Della had been through so much, yet she accomplished her dream and became a well-respected lady. She never looked back and never will. She was a fighter and had proven that Travis may have given up, but she would not. the fight was not over yet.

Sheriff Tom took a ride out to see Stewart Granger first. The telegram he got was a hard pill to swallow. He needed some help on the matter. Stewart was coming out of the barn when he saw the sheriff ride through the gate. Sheriff Tom saw him and headed his way; he told Stewart that he needed to talk. Stewart looked at Tom and knew it had to be important. He told him to step down and pull up a bale of hay.

Sheriff Tom reached into his pocket and took out the telegram and handed it to Stewart. Stewart took it and started to read. He looked up at Tom and said, "This cannot be right!" The sheriff pulled out another telegram. He said, "This is for Della."

Stewart scratched his chin and handed the telegram back to Tom and said, "No telling what Travis had said to Della in that one," as he pointed to the other paper. Stewart asked him who JD Crane was. Tom told him he was a Texas Ranger and that he was about to arrest Travis, and he smiled. Sheriff Tom told Stewart that there was trouble brewing and that Crane was the man for the job. Travis had put himself in a world of trouble, and he had to have help to get out. Sheriff Tom stood up and said that he better go and get this over with. Stewart shook his hand and said, "Best of luck."

Della was on the porch when she saw the sheriff riding in. She walked down the steps to meet him, as he reined up at the porch. He said that he hoped he was not intruding on her. Della said, "Not at all." She told him she had just brought out some lemonade and ashatf he would like a glass. Tom said, "That sounds good." Della poured the lemonade for both. He handed her a telegram. Della asked what it was. He told her it was best for her to read it, then he would explain.

Della sat down and started to read. Her hands fell onto her lap. She looked devasted. Sheriff Tom took a sip of lemonade and set his glass down. He took her by the hand and said that Travis was okay, that he was messed up inside. He told her that he was about to be arrested. Della looked up and asked why. Sheriff Tom told her it was for his own good and safety. She handed the paper back to the sheriff.

Sheriff Tom reached into his pocket and handed another piece of paper to her. He said, "This is for you from Travis." She took it with shaking hands and opened it. As she read, tears welled up in her eyes. She lay the paper down and looked at the sheriff. She said, "It may be too late. He says he does not love me, that he was sorry for all the trouble he caused me and to have a happy life. He is leaving and never coming back." Sheriff Tom told her that it was never too late. He told her not to worry about Travis. Della said, "At this point, he does not mean anything to me anymore, just a memory."

Sheriff Tom left Della with a heavy heart but knew she would be okay. Della watched him ride off and thought the fight was just beginning.

Travis had ridden out of town, figuring to camp one more night then head out to wherever his horse takes him. He would buy more supplies in the next town. He knew how to live off the land and work here and there to make it. He would be fine and stay away from towns and not get close to people. He got off his horse and set up camp. He was in deep thought when a figure walked from behind a tree and told him not to move. "Texas Ranger. You are under arrest."

Travis froze with his hand on his gun. The man told him to slowly lay his gun on the ground and step away. Travis did as he was told. The man told him to turn around. Travis turned, and the man cuffed him. He asked the man why he was being arrested. The man said, "My name is JD Cane. I am a Texas Ranger working on a case that you are involved in." Travis asked, "What case was that?" He replied, "Cal Potter." Travis said that he had done no wrong. Cane told him, "The truth is you are about to make the biggest mistake of your life." Travis said, "What mistake?" Cane said, "Della Butterfield."

Travis was numb for a moment and said, "What business is it of yours?" Cane said that he had been on the trail of Cal Potter for a while after he had killed the Smiths. He told Travis he needed his help. Travis told him that he would do what he could but may have to kill the man. Cane told him to turn around, and he took off the cuffs. He told Travis, "Let us hope it does not come to that." Travis turned and rubbed his wrists; he asked Cane if he would like some coffee and talk some more.

Sheriff Tom was riding back from his errand; the deputy met him at the door and told him he was going for lunch. Sheriff Tom told him to go on. He knew the deputy had a liking for the new cook. He sure was smitten. Deputy Eli went whistling down the street and walked in as Sally met him at the kitchen doorway with the basket of food. They both smiled at each other, and the deputy blushed as he backed out to leave. Sally waved as he left. She turned back into the kitchen; she had a thought come to her. Sally asked Rachel if it would be okay if she delivered the meals to the jailhouse every day. Rachel thought for a moment and said that was a great idea. It would give Sally a chance to have a break here and there.

The sheriff and deputy were surprised when Sally came knocking on their door later in the evening. Sally came in with all smiles with a basket of food. She told them that she would be bringing their meals daily. They already had so much to do. Sheriff Tom thanked her, and the deputy could not get a word out. Sally came daily, delivering the food basket and talking to the deputy. He was finally relaxing around her and had good visits.

Potter was restless again. His lawyer came every day. Potter did all the talking. A date for the trial had been decided. Wetherspoon was waiting for word from the judge. Potter told Wetherspoon that he needed him to do something for him. Wetherspoon asked him what he needed. Potter leaned over and told him there was a certain document that he wanted. Potter whispered to him what to do. Wetherspoon said he would take care of it; Potter told him to keep it safe until the trial, then he would tell him what to do with it. Wetherspoon nodded and left.

Potter leaned back and lay on his cot. He was tired of lying in jail and feeling sick. He would have his revenge on everyone in Rosewood and, most of all, Travis and Della. Potter turned over on his cot, feeling sluggish. He figured he overate. He would be happier if he were free.

The stage had arrived, and once the dust settled, a man stepped out and brushed off the dust. It was Judge Cartwright; he decided to come and deliver his message himself. He took his bag from the driver and started toward the sheriff's office. Sheriff Tom met him at the door, shook his hand, and said, "It was about time." The judge nodded; both men walked inside.

Potter heard voices and rolled over in his cot. He was up in a flash when he saw the judge. The judge walked over to Potter, who was up and had plenty to say. The judge told him that his day in court will be in a few days. Potter sneered and sat back on his cot.

Sally had come through the door, bringing breakfast. She stopped short at the sight of the men, but soon gathered her thoughts. She made small talk and soon was going back out the door. Sheriff Tom told the judge that Sally was the new cook over at the Rosewood Inn and that she had been bringing their daily meals. The sheriff put Potter's plate under his cell door and closed the main door behind him.

The judge said the food looked good. Sheriff Tom slapped him on the back and said, "I am buying breakfast." The judge looked at the sheriff and winked. They had to have some private talk. Both men headed the direction that Sally went.

The judge had been busy and needed to tell the sheriff what was going on. They settled at a back table and ordered breakfast. The judge set right in on what he was up to. He told Tom that there may be some trouble, and he had sent a Texas Ranger, JD Cane, to make sure that Travis Reed did not do anything foolish. Sheriff Tom laughed and said that he had just heard from him and that he had Travis under control. The judge said, "Good. Now there is another matter." He said that someone may be planning to kill Potter before his trial. Tom stopped sipping his coffee. He asked how he knew this. The judge said he got it on good authority from a reliable resource. Sheriff Tom set down his cup. He asked if the person was male or female.

Judge Cartwright said the person was not sure but that it may be a female. Sheriff Tom said, "We all may already know who it might be." The judge leaned in and asked who. Sheriff Tom said that he will check it out first before he says anything. The judge agreed and soon dug into their breakfast.

Both men talked through breakfast, not knowing they were being watched. Once they got up to leave, the sheriff made a point of sticking his head in the kitchen to tell Sally that they had enjoyed their meal, that it had been delicious. Sally was taken aback by the compliment and said that she was glad that they enjoyed it. He put his hat on as she turned to go back to work.

As they were leaving, Potter's lawyer was coming in for breakfast. They had paused. Wetherspoon was surprised to see the judge. The judge shook his hand and said that he would let him know before the week was out when the trial would be. Wetherspoon nodded and bid them good day.

The men proceeded toward the livery stable to see Doc. The sheriff knew that Potter was watching from his usual spot. Doc met them at the doorway of his office. He shook both men's hands and told them to come in. The judge said that the three of them needed to have a serious talk without prying eyes and ears. Doc told him that they came to the right place and closed the door behind them and locked it.

The judge repeated to Doc his suspicions of Potter being ambushed during or before his trial. Doc said that he had that feeling, too, and that it would be if Potter even lived before that happened. The judge looked at him and said, "What do you mean?" Sheriff cleared his throat and told the judge that when Potter had kidnapped Nellie, she had put a poison in the salve she used on his wound. Potter was slowly dying inside. The sheriff went on to say that under the circumstances that Nellie was in, he did not blame her.

The judge said that he would set the trial for the coming week on Monday early morning. He looked at the sheriff and Doc and said that if Potter dies, it would be in prison. Both men agreed. The judge said that he would tell Wetherspoon and Langford about the date. He looked at the sheriff and told him to be sure to have more guards this time. He did not want anything to go wrong. The sheriff said he was already ready.

After Wetherspoon finished his breakfast, which was quick, he went to see Potter. Potter was waiting for him and asked him if he had done what he was told to do. Wetherspoon wiped his brow and said, "Yes, I have what you wanted." Potter said, "Good. Do not open it or let anyone know that you have it. Your family's lives are at stake." Wetherspoon nodded and left.

Potter started coughing and went to his bunk. He did not feel very well. He rubbed his wound and felt anger. He was a man that wanted revenge. He could see nothing else.

Nancy Robertson, the new cook at Coyote Springs, had taken a liking to Della. As Nellie did in the past, she kept a close watch on Della. Della had kept busy and enjoyed her many visits from Autumn and Nellie. She made sure that on Sundays, it was for friends and family to visit and to laugh.

Business was good, and an endless stream of lodgers came and went. The mine was still producing. Silas and his men took care of that. He was still upset with his son. The boy needed to forget the past and move on.

Silas had talked to Sparrow to get things off his chest. Sparrow told him that we all have demons and deal with them as we can. Travis was young and had a lot to learn. Silas said he may be young, but he was bullheaded. Sparrow laughed. "In time, he will face his past, then he will be able to take his future." Silas agreed.

JD Crane and Travis had been riding for a few days. They were headed back to Coyote Springs. JD had asked Travis if there was somewhere they could hold up and not be seen until the trial. Travis looked at him and said, "I know of a place, but why do we need to stay low?" JD told him he had his orders and would not go against them. Travis told him, "I know the perfect place."

Travis led JD to the entrance of the cave. They saw that it had been boarded up. They dismounted and started taking the boards down to gain entrance. They soon moved their horses inside. Travis told JD that this was where Potter had kept Della captive until she escaped. They unsaddled the horses and settled in. JD made sure they had enough provisions to last for a while. He did not want to be seen; he knew that he had to keep Travis at bay.

Later that evening, a visitor came to the mouth of the cave. An old friend trotted off into the darkness. Later, JD raised his head from his bed as he heard the coyote howl. Travis told him it was an old friend welcoming him home. JD turned and called it a night. There was only the light of the fire and the coyotes playing in the night. Travis smiled. He was home.

The Rosewood Inn was busy with a nice flow of diners. Sheriff Tom had brought his wife, Sue, and their two boys for supper. Stewart and Julia Granger were at their usual table. The judge came downstairs to the dining room when Jim Langford came through the door. The judge stopped and greeted Jim; he asked him to join him for supper. Both men turned to go into the dining room. Rachel greeted the two men and showed them to a table.

Back in the kitchen, Sally was busy at the stove. She was trying to concentrate on her orders. Rachel came in and told her that the dining room was full. Sally turned and dropped a pan to the floor. She reached down to clean up her mess, Rachel asked her if she was okay. Sally told her she was simply fine, just excited about being so busy. Rachel patted her on the shoulder and told her it was because of her fine cooking. Sally smiled, pleased at her words, and went back to her task.

Rachel went from table to table to talk with her patrons. She was pleased that business had picked up. Hank Sanders was also pleased; the hotel had been booked for weeks.

Wetherspoon came downstairs to have supper. When he got to the dining room, he saw that it was full. Rachel came up to him and told him that every table was full, and he would have to share. Wetherspoon was about to turn away when the judge asked him to come and join him and Jim Langford. Wetherspoon went reluctantly to their table and sat down. The judge told the men that he wanted to tell them that the trial was set for Monday morning the coming week. Both lawyers said they would be ready.

Sally was helping Rachel bring out some of the plates to the patrons. She stopped short when she came through the kitchen door, surprised that there were so many people. She caught herself and walked over to the sheriff's table with their supper. Sheriff Tom told her, "Thank you," and introduced his wife, Sue, to her. Sally relaxed and smiled and chatted a bit. She returned to the kitchen and brought out another tray. She carried this one to the table where the Grangers were sitting. She smiled and placed their food in front of them. They said, "Thank you," and she returned to the kitchen.

Sally went back into the kitchen out of breath, but excited. She really liked her job here, and the people were all so nice. She thought she would just stay awhile after her work was done.

Julia touched Stewart's arm and told him in a whisper that she had seen Sally somewhere before, yet she was not sure where. Stewart told her that it would come to her later. Julia said, "I am sure it would."

C H A P T E R **16**

Morning came early. Rachel came downstairs to the dining room, then into the kitchen. She stopped short. The kitchen was dark and cold. There was no Sally. She turned and went up to Sally's room, but she was not there. The room was empty. She hurried back downstairs; she told Hank that Sally was gone. Rachel said that she had work to do. It was going to be a long day. Hank shook his head and went back to his desk.

Doc had awoken with Jim knocking on his door. Doc asked Jim what in the world was the matter. Jim said that Ms. Sally's horse was gone! Doc put his pants on and went into the livery to check the stall. Sure enough, the horse was gone. Doc finished getting dressed and walked over to see the sheriff. Hank Sanders was going his way too. Sheriff Tom was coming up the alley when he saw the two men and asked what got them out so early. Hank started first. He said that Sally had left during the night. Doc said, "Well, that answered his problem of a missing horse."

Sheriff Tom said, "Well, looks like we lost a good cook." Both men agreed and turned to go about their day. He stood for a moment, watching the men leave. He had been right about his hunch. He would see the judge.

When Doc got back to the livery, Jim was hitching up the buggy. Doc told him that Sally had left during the night; Jim scratched his head, glad it was not stolen. Doc agreed and went in to make him some coffee. Jim continued his task and told Doc he was going to breakfast. Doc waved him off.

The judge was having breakfast in the corner. He saw Jim walk in and nodded. Sheriff Tom came in right behind him, saw the judge, and went straight to his table. The sheriff asked the judge if he heard the news about Sally. He said yes. Rachel walked over to the table and took his order and filled their cups. Both men expressed how sorry they were about Sally running out on her. Rachel said, "Thank you. Life goes on." She turned and went back into the kitchen.

Jim had finished his meal and soon left, heading toward the livery. His day was about to start. He told Doc he was back and heading out. Doc told him to make sure to tell Della hello for him. Jim said, "Sure thing," and soon he had the buggy heading out. He had the horse at a smooth trot, and once he got close to Coyote Springs, he took a side road that went to the mine. He pulled up in front of Silas and Autumn's home. Silas came out to greet him. Jim said that he had wanted to stop by and say how much he appreciated the care that he had gotten from Autumn and how much their friendship meant to him. Silas shook his hand. Autumn had come to the porch and waved as Jim turned the buggy to leave.

Jim drove the buggy through the gates of Coyote Springs. It had grown so much since Della had bought the place. He pulled up to the porch. He was picking up a couple of the guests that were checking out. Della came out to greet him. She asked if he had breakfast yet. He tipped his hat and told her he had. He told her that Doc sent his best. She told Jim to tell Doc to come on Sunday for lunch and for him to come too. The guests were coming out, and Jim loaded their luggage and helped them into the buggy. He told Della that they would come. He said, "Before I forget, Ms. Rachel lost her cook, Sally, who left during the night." Della told him that she had not heard, and she waved him off.

Della went back into the house; she went upstairs to prepare the room that her guest had just checked out of. She busied herself, humming as she went. Soon her task was completed, and she made her way to the kitchen. Nancy turned as she came in and asked if she needed to fix Jim some breakfast. Della smiled and said no but that to expect him Sunday for lunch. Nancy was smiling big and started humming. Della had a feeling the two liked each other. She turned and went about her work.

Travis and JD were making breakfast. They heard a noise that sounded like a bird. JD reached for his gun when Travis grabbed his arm. He told him to hold on. Travis returned the sound, as he crept toward the entrance. JD was close behind. When Travis stopped short, he told JD to relax. Travis walked out of the opening and came face-to-face with Sparrow. Sparrow said, "I thought it was you. Who is with you?" Travis turned and told JD that this was his uncle. He told Sparrow to climb down to talk. Travis told his uncle that he could not tell anyone they were there. Sparrow told him he would keep his word; JD asked him if he would do something for him, and he gave him a piece of paper. He asked Sparrow to give it to the sheriff. Sparrow took it and said he would get it to him. The men stood up, and Sparrow touched Travis's shoulder and told him that it was good he was home. Travis said that he was too.

Sparrow had been out riding when he saw the entrance to the cave had been disturbed. He had a feeling that Travis may have come back. That was why he whistled like a bird; he had taught Travis many things when he was younger. He looked at the note and headed into town.

Della had finished her morning duties, and Nancy was preparing lunch. There was a knock at the door. It was Julia Granger; Della opened the door and greeted her with open arms and asked her to come in. Julia said that she had come by for a visit, Della told her she was just in time for lunch. She led Julia to the dining room. As Nancy was setting the table, she asked her to place another plate because she had a guest. Della asked Julia to have a seat and to fill her in on all her news.

They had a lot of catching up to do. Julia was beaming and so happy to be home. Julia told Della she was saddened to hear that Travis had left her and hoped that he would return. Della told her that Travis was fighting his own battles, and she was not one of them. Julia changed the subject and asked her if she had heard about Rachel Sander's cook, Sally, leaving in the night. Della told her that Jim had given her the news this morning. Nancy brought in lunch, and the ladies were enjoying it. Julia went on to say that she had seen the woman somewhere before. Della asked her why it bothered her. She said, "Because I saw her in New Orleans about the time Cal Potter was there."

Julia went on to say that she was a cook at the hotel where she was staying. She had felt like she was following Potter. Della told her that she never heard Sally being mentioned at all by Potter. Julia said that there was no connection, but it was odd she showed up in Rosewood and then left in the night. Della agreed, and they finished their lunch. They went to the porch and sat a while longer. Soon, Julia said she had to go and was off.

Della lingered on the porch and looked to the hilltop; she stood up for a moment when she thought she saw someone. She turned and told herself that it was long ago. The figure on the hilltop was gone, but would return in the coming days, waiting.

Sparrow had made it into town and rode up to the sheriff's office. Sheriff Tom was just coming out when he saw Sparrow. Sparrow did not get off his horse. He just told the sheriff he had a note for him, and then he rode off. Sheriff Tom opened the note and read what was inside. He thought, *Great timing*, and put the note in his pocket and sat back in his chair.

Wetherspoon was inside visiting Potter, who was asking all kinds of questions. Wetherspoon told him that the judge had set the trial for Monday morning at nine o'clock. Potter asked him if he was ready. Wetherspoon just said yes. Potter went into a coughing spell and told him to leave and come back tomorrow. Potter was not feeling nor looking too well.

Jim Langford walked down to the livery and asked Jim to drive him out to Coyote Springs. Jim told him he would, and soon the two were headed out of town. The two men chatted on the drive. Langford had not been to Coyote Springs in a while, and as they rode through the gates, he was surprised. Jim pulled up to the porch, and Langford stepped down. Della came from the side of the house, pleased to see them. Jim headed to the kitchen as Della went up the steps with her lawyer. She asked him to have a seat.

Della looked at him and told him that it was time. He said, "Yes, it is." Della said, "I am ready to get this over with." She went on to say that she wished Travis had not left like he did. Jim said that Travis must have had his reasons. Della said, "Yes, he did, and the wrong ones." Della told her lawyer that she wanted a chance to speak at the trial. Jim looked at her and thought it would be unwise. Della told him that she had things to say and that she was not scared of Potter anymore.

They talked awhile about other things. He told her that Coyote Springs had grown since he had been out. Della said, "Yes, a lot of hard work and determination." Jim had told her the trial was set for Monday morning at nine o'clock. Della said she would be in town the day before and would stay with Ms. Nancy. As if on cue, Jim came out of the house with a covered plate and a big smile. Jim Langford stood and said, "Now there is a happy man." Della laughed, a happy woman in the kitchen. Della sent them off with a wave as she turned to go in. She was feeling peaceful and went inside.

News traveled fast in a small town; the trial was coming. Sheriff Tom put the word out that he needed deputies, and soon he had plenty. Granger had sent his best men, and Sparrow had wanted to help; all were good, trustworthy men.

CHAPTER 17

Sally had left during the night; she was scared and had not gone too far. She had liked the town and especially Rachel Sanders. Sally was feeling lost. She spent the night in the woods and was hungry and cold. She had heard a noise on the road and looked to see that it was a buggy going by. She got on her horse and started in the direction that it came from. She came upon Coyote Springs. She stopped her horse. She made the decision to ride on down.

Della had come back to the porch to retrieve a tray she had left when she saw a rider coming through the gate. She waited to see who it was and was surprised to see a woman. The woman rode up and asked her if she could have some water. Della said, "Of course," and went to get her some. When Della came back out, the woman was sitting on her steps. Della sat beside her and gave her water, which she had drank quickly. Della could see she was in a bad way and helped her to a chair on the porch.

The woman told her name was Sally and that she was in trouble. She started to spill everything out to Della. Della sat and listened and soon understood. Sally told her that it was wrong what she did, but he had to pay. Della told her that she understood and that she was welcome to stay with her. No one would bother her. Sally was so drained that she was relieved. Della told her that she needed food and a bath, and they would talk more later. Della went to the side of the porch and hollered at Randy Crow to get the horse and take care of it. Della turned and took Sally into the house. When Randy came up to retrieve the horse, she asked him to get Julia Granger and Nellie as soon as he could and no one else. He nodded and left.

Della took Sally into the house. She hollered at Nancy that she needed to fix a plate for Sally and warm water for a bath. Sally was so tired, yet she felt safe. She ate hungrily. Soon, Della showed her to a room where a bath was waiting, Nancy had laid out fresh clothes for her. Della left her for her bath.

It was not long before Nellie and Julia came through the door, wondering what in the world was going on. Della looked at Julia and said that she had found the missing cook. Julia said, "Oh my." Nellie looked puzzled; Della told the women to go into the parlor where she followed them. Della told them what Sally had done to Potter and why. The women just sat and looked at each other. Sally walked into the room.

Sally stepped back to leave, but Della told her, "We are all friends here. Please come sit beside me." Della told Sally her story, then Nellie and Julia finished. Sally was not the only one who had come across Cal Potter. Della said, "Ladies, we have things to discuss before Monday. Who is with me?" It was decided that Sally would stay with Della and that no one would know she was here.

Julia said that she would fill Stewart in on what was going on and that they would come to the trial early one day. Della told them that each of them would testify against Potter. it was their right to do so. Nellie said she would also tell Sam. Della said, "Good, then we all know what we need to do. No matter what, Potter will go to prison or die before the trial. Either way, we will be justified." The women nodded in agreement. They all took turns hugging each other. They were strong women.

After the women left, Sally sat longer and talked with Della. She asked her if things did not work out in town after the trial, she could stay on with her and work. Della told her that she would have her old job back, and yes, if it did not work out, she was more than welcome to stay. Sally smiled.

Julia went home and told Stewart that she had been right about seeing the cook, Sally. She told him of her visit with Della. He sat back and thought that Potter was in for a shocking surprise come Monday. He told Julia whatever she needed to let him know. She said that they would go into Rosewood the day before and get a room where they would hide Sally. Della would be bringing her; Della was staying with Ms. Nancy. Julia said that they all would be testifying.

Travis and JD were at odds from time to time. Travis would wander off to the hill to look down on Coyote Springs, and JD would go after him. Travis was restless, and JD knew it. Sparrow rode by and told them that he had delivered the note and that the trial was Monday at nine o'clock. JD told him, "Thanks." Travis said, "We will be there."

Della and Sally bonded like sisters. They talked for hours. Nancy came and joined them. It was a nice afternoon. Soon the women went to their rooms for the evening. Della had a lot of thinking to do, and Sally wanted to just sleep.

Potter was trying to sleep, but he was in pain. He yelled out several times. Deputy Eli told the sheriff he would get Doc; the sheriff said it was a good idea. The deputy went to get Doc to look at Potter. Doc hurried over as soon as he could. Doc went back to see Potter and saw him tossing and turning in his cot. Doc told him to be still and let him look at him. Potter was mumbling. Doc did all he could and gave Potter some pills to take. Doc turned to the sheriff and shook his head.

Doc walked all the way out the door before he told the sheriff that it is not looking good for his prisoner. The sheriff asked, "How long does he have?" Doc shrugged and walked off. The sheriff went back in and told Eli to just keep him comfortable. It was going to be a long night for the deputy.

Come morning, Potter was a little better. He barely ate his breakfast. The deputy was stretching in his chair when the sheriff walked in. The deputy told him that it had been a long night but that Potter had slept some. The sheriff told his deputy to go home and get some sleep. He walked back and looked in on Potter, lying on his bunk, and shook his head as he closed the door.

Wetherspoon came in a little early to visit Potter. The sheriff told him that he had had a rough night and that it would be best if he came back later. Wetherspoon told him that he would and left, relieved. He wanted to get this trial over as soon as possible, then he would pack his family up and move far away.

The last few days went fast. It was Sunday. The sheriff had planned that all the deputies would come in and get their instructions on where each one would be posted. The men had arrived early and were ready to go. Potter was up by then and trying to listen. He was not able to hear much, for he had another coughing spree, and it left him weak.

The sheriff told his deputies to walk over to the Desert Rose saloon. He showed each man where to be and that they had orders not to move and be alert. He double-checked the back way out of the saloon and told Jed that he wanted the door locked from the inside. Jed told him that he would go ahead and do it. Sheriff Tom told his men that there would be only one way in and one way out.

Jed had been cleaning up the saloon and setting up the chairs. Ms. Nancy came in and out to make sure he was doing it right. The sheriff had left with his men. The Desert Rose would not be in business today. Ms. Nancy was going with Doc to see Della. This she did every Sunday.

Della and Nancy were getting ready for their guest. Sally came downstairs and helped. Della told her that she should join them today. Sally asked if that would be wise. She just smiled and said it would. Sally felt good inside. She told Sally that she was going to tell them that you were a friend of mine that dropped in for a visit.

Soon there were buggies coming through the gate. Della was on the porch, waiting for them. She had Sally beside her. As they had reined up and were stepping down, they came up the steps, and Della greeted them and introduced Sally. Julia had a big smile and went along with Della as did Nellie. Doc had brought a bottle of wine to celebrate.

Everyone was in a great mood and talked about pleasant things. Della told Nancy that she was joining them today and was to sit by Jim. Nancy smiled and continued bringing out the food, with Nellie and Della's help. Della sat at the end of the table and looked around at all her friends.

She stood as Doc had filled their wineglasses, and she said that she would like to say a few words to them. Everyone turned to listen to Della. She told them that each of them had touched her life in some way, both good and bad. It made her stronger and that she loved every one of them. They were her family and would always be. She went on to say that tomorrow would be a fresh start for all of them.

Della sat back down, and Stewart Granger stood up with glass in hand. He looked at Della and said that if it had not been for her, he would not have his Julia back and found a very dear friend. "I would like to make a toast to you, Della. May you live long and be happy in all you do and that one day, you, too, will have your loved one back." Everyone stood up and toasted Della, who had tears in her eyes. She told them, "Thank you," and to eat before the food got cold. Soon everyone had to leave for Rosewood, for the trial was in the morning.

Chapter **18**

After everyone left, Della, Nancy, and Sally cleaned up. Della had given Nancy instructions on what to do. She left them to go upstairs and pack. Sally came up to help. She sat on the bed and talked with Della. Della told her that she would ride into town as planned and hide until the trial started. Jim was returning to pick her up to take her to Ms. Nancy.

Sally took Della's bag and hers down and put them on the porch. She saw Jim coming and went to get Della. Jim reined up and got her bags and put them in the buggy as Della came out. Della told Jim that Sally was coming with them and that it was especially important that he not say a word to anyone. Jim nodded and knew that she was the missing cook but had not said anything. Soon they were headed to Rosewood.

Rosewood Inn was remarkably busy. The Grangers, Nellie, and Sam had checked in. Della arrived later and had Jim hold up outside of town for Sally to get out. Sally knew where to go because Julia was waiting for her. Jim flicked the reins and was soon in front of the Desert Rose. He helped Della out of the buggy and gave her bag. Ms. Nancy came out to greet her. Jim left them as they walked in. Sally had made it to the back door of the inn. Julia was waiting and slipped her upstairs.

Wetherspoon went back to see Potter, who was up, and they went over what Wetherspoon was supposed to do. Potter sat back, thinking he was ready. His lawyer left to go back to his room. Everyone in Rosewood was settling down for the evening, waiting for the trial to be held in the morning.

Morning came quickly, Della was nervous yet determined to be strong. Today was her day. The judge had gotten up early and had his breakfast. He soon made his way to the Desert Rose, where Jed let him in. The judge wanted to double-check everything, but he knew that the sheriff already had it under control.

Jed brought the judge a cup of coffee. The two men talked a bit, then Jed went and unlocked the front door. The lawyers and the sheriff were coming in to see the judge. Sheriff Tom told the judge that when his deputies arrived, he would be bringing Potter over from the jail. The judge told him that would be good.

Wetherspoon and Langford set up their tables and were preparing for the trial, both men intent at what they were doing. Wetherspoon was nervous but tried not to show it. The deputies had arrived, and he told them to take their places, and he took the two who would be guarding Potter.

The sheriff and the deputies went to the jail. Deputy Eli took the keys off the peg to get Potter out of his cell. Potter heard him coming and stood up. He was ready. He turned and put his hands behind his back as the deputy put the handcuffs on. He took Potter by the arm and led him out. Potter came face-to-face with the sheriff and the other deputies. He had a smirk on his face as they led him out onto the street.

It was a sight to see armed men walking a handcuffed man down the street. They came to the saloon, and a deputy that was inside opened the door to let them in. Potter was led up to where Wetherspoon was sitting, and his two guards stood behind him. Wetherspoon got more nervous. Potter leaned over and whispered something to him. He just patted his briefcase. Potter relaxed and kept the smirky smile on his face.

Soon the courtroom was filling up. The sheriff made sure that the Grangers and Nellie with Sam sat up front. Della and Ms. Nancy had come in and sat beside them. Della sat by Julia, who took her by the hand and squeezed it. The courtroom had filled up fast and had to leave the saloon doors open. There were two guards at the door.

Jim Langford walked over to Della and asked her to come sit by him; Della stood and went with him. They were soon in quiet conversation; Langford would nod his head as Della talked. Potter was taking all this in. Langford knew that Della was in control and was not worried about the outcome at all.

The judge called the court to order. Everyone quieted down. The judge went on to say, "Today, everyone would hold their tongues unless they were on the witness stand." If not, then he pointed to the guards around the room and said, "They will escort you out for good."

The judge looked at each of the lawyers and asked them if they were ready to proceed. They stood and said that they were ready. As they sat back down, the judge went on to say that the accused, Cal Potter, and the defendant, Della Butterfield, were in court. He concluded that the trial was ready to begin.

The judge hit his gavel on the table and said that he called this court to order. He asked Jim Langford to call his first witness. Langford stood and said he would like to call Sally Anderson to the stand. Everyone was looking around, looking for her when she walked into the room from Ms. Nancy's apartments. She went straight to the chair where Langford was waiting. She stood and put her hand on the Bible and swore to tell the truth, the whole truth, then she sat down.

Everyone was waiting for her to speak; Potter had no idea who she was and why she was a witness. Langford asked her why she was here to testify against Cal Potter. Sally looked at Langford, then she turned to the court and spoke. She said that her name was not Sally Anderson, but that it was Sally Muldoon. She was the sister of Gracie Muldoon. The courtroom erupted. The judge used the gavel, and it got quiet. She went on to say that she had been following Potter for quite some time, and she said that she had wanted him to pay for killing her sister. When he left New Orleans, she followed and was lucky to have gotten a job at the Rosewood Inn.

Sally looked at the Sanderses and went on to say that she grew to love Rosewood and the people here. She had liked her job. She said she was sorry for misleading everyone and taking off in the night. She paused; Langford asked her how she planned to kill Cal Potter. Sally looked at him and took a deep breath. She said that she had asked

Ms. Rachel if she could take food to the jail, so she did daily. She went on to say that she wanted to make sure that Potter got the right plate. Langford asked her, "Why was that?" She looked at Cal Potter and said, "Because I put a poison in his food, so he would die a slow death."

The room was silent, but Potter had jumped up, calling her all kinds of nasty things. A guard made him sit back down. Langford asked to go on. Sally took a deep breath and said that she was not sorry for what she had done and that she would gladly pay for her actions. Langford said he had no more questions. The judge asked Wetherspoon if he had any. Wetherspoon looked at Potter, who shook his head no. Wetherspoon told the judge he did not. The judge asked Sally to step down and not to leave the courtroom. She went and sat by Julia, who took her by the hand and squeezed it hard.

The judge asked if Langford had another witness. Langford stood and said, "Yes, I call Nellie Oaks to the stand." Nellie stood up and walked to the stand. Langford swore her in, and she sat in the chair. Langford asked her why she wanted to testify today. Nellie said that she wanted to tell what she had done to Cal Potter. Langford told her to go on. She said that after Potter had kidnapped Della that he had paid a visit to Stewart Granger and got shot. Potter had kidnapped her so she could tend to his gunshot wound. Langford said, "And what did you do?" Nellie went on to say that she had done what he told her to do, but that she had put poison in the salve she used to put on the stitches, then bandaged it up.

Potter again got up and was cursing. He told her that he was going to get her and the Sally girl too. A guard had to restrain him so he could not get up again. The judge hit his gavel and called order. Nellie had composed herself, and she looked at Cal Potter and told him that he was no good and would do it again! The courtroom cheered, the judge pointed his gavel, and it got quiet.

Langford asked Nellie if she had anything else to say. She said, "Yes, as I said, I am not sorry for what I did. He kidnapped me and tried to kill me by burning down a house where I was locked in a room. He deserves to be punished." Langford told the judge that he had no more questions. Wetherspoon nodded that he had none.

Nellie stepped off the stand and went and squeezed Della's hand and went to sit by Sam. Langford called Julia Granger to the stand. She stood and walked up to Langford. He swore her in, and she sat down. Langford also asked her why she was here to testify against Cal Potter. Julia said that she wanted to have her say as Nellie as he had tried to kill her in the same house fire. She said that she had come to Rosewood using a false name because she wanted to know if her husband, Stewart Granger, had changed. She had heard that Cal Potter had made trouble here but felt no danger from him until her drive out to the house that Stewart had built for her.

CHAPTER 19

Julia was finishing her testimony. She said that in a way it had brought her husband back to her, but that Cal Potter needed to pay for all the harm he had caused. Langford said he had no more questions. Wetherspoon again said he had none, and Julia stepped down.

Potter was sitting, fuming at his lawyer; he wanted his turn. Langford stood and told the judge that he would call Della Butterfield to the stand. He went on to say that Della would speak in her own words her testimony against Cal Potter. Della stood and walked up to the stand where she was sworn in. Della sat down and looked straight at Potter; her eyes did not leave him. Potter shifted in his chair.

Langford told Della that she may begin. She looked at her lawyer for a moment, then her eyes went back to Potter, and she began to speak. Potter was on the edge of his seat, waiting to hear what she had to say. The room was noticeably quiet, then she began to speak, Della said that she had been through so much torture from this man, and most of her friends have also. She went on to say that she was weak before and knew she had grown stronger. When Potter had her chained to a post in a cave to die, she got her strength from inside herself. She knew that she was the only one that was going to save her.

She continued night and day and made the post move. She said that she had strength enough to escape. Now she understood why it was so easy for her to chain Potter up to the same post she had escaped from. She looked at Nellie and smiled. Della turned to look at Potter. She went on to say that she had to escape before Potter came back. She had done something that would make him terribly angry and would have killed her on the spot.

She said, "Potter, remember you had beat me to sign a marriage certificate?" Potter tried to stand but could not. Della said, "Did you even look at my signature?" Wetherspoon, as if on cue, got the document for Potter to look at. Potter was furious! Della said that he got what he wanted. He was married but not to her, but to Gracie Muldoon.

The courtroom erupted again then quieted down, for they were hanging on to every word Della was saying. Della kept looking at Potter, who had slumped in his chair, a beaten man. Della said, "Sally, Nellie, Julia, and I were abused by you, yet we each were strong enough to do what we had to do to bring you down. You had taken our loved ones from us and put wedges between those who matter the most. You will be sentenced to prison, but you will slowly die knowing who did it to you. Our revenge is complete."

Della turned to the judge and asked him to not be hard on Sally, that she would take responsibility of her. The judge told her that he would see what he could do, then he looked at Langford and asked him if he was finished with this witness. Langford said he was. Wetherspoon was done and glad of it. The judge told Della she could step down. A voice in the courtroom said that she was not finished.

Della turned, as everyone else did, to the voice. It was Travis, standing in the doorway with JD Crane behind him. The judge said, "Order," and told the men to step forward. JD Crane told the judge that he was delivering a prisoner as ordered. They had stopped in front of the judge, who had a smile on his face. He told the ranger to remove the cuffs. Potter looked up at Travis and became furious.

The judge said, "Did I hear you that this witness was not finished with her testimony?" Travis said, "Yes, sir, she is not." Della was in shock to see Travis. He looked rough, but his eyes were clear. She prepared herself for whatever he had to say.

The judge said that the witness was his and sat back. Travis cleared his throat. He looked at Della. "Answer a question for me." Della looked at him and said, "Now what would that be?" Travis said, "You say you are stronger from your ordeal." She answered,

"Yes." "Then how strong are you to forgive me for running out on you?" Della turned to him and began to speak. "Travis Reed, how dare you ask me that question. You ran away from me. You were the one that was not strong enough to fight for me! You had as much revenge in you as Cal Potter sitting there, ready to die!" Della was furious! Travis knew he hit a nerve. "Then you still love me." Della said, "Love? You do not know what love is! Have you sat night after night, crying your eyes out for someone, worrying about if they were okay or not!" Travis said, "Then you do love me." Della just sat and looked at him. The judge told her that she was under oath and had to tell the truth. Della sighed and looked at Travis and said yes.

Travis said that he could not hear her. She stood and shouted at Travis, "Yes, I do!" Travis came around to her and bent down and looked up at her as he took her hand and said, "Della Butterfield, would you marry this worthless coward of a man?" Della took his hand and looked him in the eyes and said, "Yes, I will."

The judge hit his gavel to the table and said that court was adjourned! The whole courtroom had erupted again. Della and Travis were wrapped in each other's arms, and he then kissed her long and hard.

Potter just sat in his chair a beat man. Wetherspoon got up and left him sitting there. The guards were picking Potter up out of his chair, then Potter made a dash toward Travis and Della. He had pulled Travis's gun and pointed at them. Travis moved in front of Della, but it was too late. A shot had been fired. Everyone hit the floor and came up to see Potter on the floor. Travis turned to see Della with her gun drawn. She had fired the shot. She looked at Travis. She put her gun away. She told him that a lot of things had changed since he had been gone.

Travis took her by the arm, as Doc came to check Potter. He was just wounded; the two deputies took him back to jail. Doc said he would be there in a bit to dress the wound. He looked at the judge and asked him if he was in a hurry. The judge smiled and said that he was not. Doc looked at Della and Travis then turned to everyone in the room. Doc said in a loud voice and said, "Sorry, folks, but the trial is over, and now there was going to be a wedding."

Travis and Della were ready. They stood in front of Judge Cartwright as he pronounced them man and wife. The judge turned to Ms. Nancy and asked her to open the bar. Drinks were on him. Jed was soon filling glasses. Travis and Della were lost in each other.

Stewart and Julia hugged each other, glad that the two were finally together. Nellie was crying happily, and Sam held her close. Sally was happy, too, glad that she had come clean with what she had done. Della had stood up for her, and that meant a lot. Rachel and Hank Sanders came up to Sally. At first, it was awkward, then Rachel just gave Sally a hug. Rachel told Sally that her job was waiting if she still wanted it. Sally looked at them both and said, "Do I ever!"

Autumn and Silas were both beaming and had gone and gave them each a hug. Autumn drew her son to the side and told him that she was glad he came around. Travis just smiled and said, "I had lots of help." JD Crane held up a glass to Travis. Travis nodded to him.

Doc and the judge were happy that the trial was over, justice done, and new lives beginning again. What a day. Doc left and went to check on Potter. Deputy Eli met him at the door and told him to hurry. Doc went in and saw that Potter was not moving. Doc checked his pulse and found that he was dead. Doc shook his head and said, "Yes, justice is done."

Later that evening, Travis and Della arrived at Coyote Springs, their home, both feeling so alive and full of love. Nancy had seen them come through the gates and ran to the porch to greet them. Travis jumped out of the buggy and whirled Della around in happiness. Nancy was laughing and saying, "Della, glad you are home." Travis set Della down. She caught her breath and told Nancy that this was Travis, that the trial was over, and that they had won. Then she showed Nancy her hand,. Della said that Travis and she are finally married. Nancy gave Della a big hug, Travis retrieved Della's bags, and they went inside.

Nancy had prepared supper and started setting the table. They heard voices coming up the porch. It was Della's family. Everyone had come to celebrate. Jim had brought Doc and Ms. Nancy, and close behind were Nellie and Sam. The Grangers were arriving too. Sally had hitched a ride with Doc and Ms. Nancy. Della was beaming.

She had Travis sit at the head of the table. Everyone laughed and drank the wine that Doc had brought. Della looked around at her family. It was complete. As the evening progressed, everyone headed home. Travis and Della, arm in arm, waved their family off. They turned toward the barn and went for a walk as they did long ago. This time, it was different. This time, it would be forever. They stopped. Travis bent to kiss Della, and they looked to the hilltop toward the sound of coyotes. They both laughed, and Travis kissed her. He kept kissing her as the coyotes howled their approval.

About the Author

Gail Odom West lives in Texas with her husband and has a lake as her backyard.

She enjoys fishing and working in her garden. She also enjoys canning from her garden, and she is a herbalist. Between her husband and she, they have five children, six grandchildren, and two great-grandchildren.